Word Master

Seeing and Using Words

LEVEL 9

Lessons 1- 30

Series Designer
Philip J. Solimene

Editors
Janice Colby Solimene
Joyce W. Masterson
Laura Solimene

Consultant
Douglas P. Barnard, Ed.D

Author
David L. Bacon

EDCON PUBLISHING GROUP
www.edconpublishing.com

EDCON Publishing Group

30 Montauk Blvd. Oakdale NY 11769
info@edconpublishing.com
www.edconpublishing.com
1-888-553-3266 Fax 1-888-518-1564

Printed in U.S.A.
ISBN# 0-931334-41-1

CONTENTS

INTRODUCTION

What do you do when you see a word you do not know? Do you use a dictionary to learn its meaning, do you look at the parts of the word to find a "root" word, or do you try to understand the word's meaning from its context?

New words can be learned in different ways. One good way to understand the meaning of a word is to understand what it means in the sentence or paragraph where it is used. To do this, you must understand the meaning of the sentence or paragraph you are reading.

However, understanding a word in context will not always teach you all you should know about the word. A dictionary will be needed for you to learn how to pronounce the word and to learn the word's meaning or meanings.

This book will help you to:

1. Learn the use of context clues
2. Learn the use of a dictionary
3. Learn the different forms of words

THE WAY TO USE THIS BOOK

Look at the CONTENTS page (page iii). The large black type will show you the four main parts of the book: SEQUENCE 9-1 through SEQUENCE 9-30, EXERCISE G, ANSWER KEY, and PROGRESS CHART.

Then, turn to SEQUENCE 9-1. Look at the four pages that make up SEQUENCE 9-1. Every sequence in the book is similar. Every sequence has six sections that follow one another:

A Writing the Words
B Using Context Clues
C Checking the Meaning
D Completing the Sentences
E Using the Skill
F Supplementary Writing Exercise

A seventh section

G Sentences for Spelling Exercise

Use CONTENTS page to locate sentences for Spelling Exercise.

Instructions for each of these sections are on the next page.

Your teacher will provide instruction in rules for recognizing and spelling different forms of words.

A WRITING THE WORDS

1. Write the word you see to the left of the blank lines, beginning with number 1.
2. Say each word after you write it.
3. Follow the instructions for part B of this section.

B USING CONTEXT CLUES

1. At the top of the page are entries as they appear in a dictionary. Read the entries and their meanings. All the words will be used in some of the exercises. If you have trouble pronouncing a word, use the Pronunciation Key on the inside of the back cover of this book.
2. Follow the instructions for the exercise. When you have completed the exercise, check your answers with the Answer Key.

C CHECKING THE MEANING

Follow the instructions for the exercise. When you have completed the exercise, check your answers with the Answer Key.

D COMPLETING THE SENTENCES

Follow the instructions for the exercise. When you have completed the exercise, check your answers with the Answer Key. Enter your score on the Progress Chart.

E USING THE SKILL

Follow the instructions for the exercise. When you have completed the exercise, check your answers with the Answer Key. Enter your score on the Progress Chart.

F SUPPLEMENTARY WRITING EXERCISE

Follow the instructions for the exercise. There is no Answer Key for this exercise. Your teacher will check your work.

G SENTENCES FOR SPELLING EXERCISE

1. Each sentence in this exercise contains one of your new words. The new words are underlined.
2. Two or three days after you have completed the four pages of exercises for one sequence, your teacher may want to know how well you have learned the new words. The teacher may pronounce the new word, then read the sentence that uses the word, then pronounce the word again.
3. You are to write the word on a separate sheet of paper. Enter your score on the Progress Chart. Then correct any mistakes you made.
4. You might be asked to use the sentences in this exercise to give a spelling test to someone else.

A WRITING THE WORDS

A. Write these words on the blank lines.
Then say each word.

	Write
monologue	1. ____________
monolith	2. ____________
monogamy	3. ____________
monochromatic	4. ____________
biased	5. ____________
biannual	6. ____________
biennial	7. ____________
triarchy	8. ____________
triennial	9. ____________
triangle	10. ____________

B. Each word begins with a prefix.
Write the prefix for each word.

1. ____________
2. ____________
3. ____________
4. ____________
5. ____________
6. ____________
7. ____________
8. ____________
9. ____________
10. ____________

THESE PREFIXES HAVE MEANINGS THAT RELATE TO **NUMBERS**.

SEQUENCE 9-1

bi- *prefix* [ME, fr. L; akin to OE *twi-*] **1 a** : two <*bi*parous> **b** : coming or occurring every two <*bi*monthly> <*bi*weekly> **c** : into two parts <*bi*sect> **2 a** : twice : doubly : on both sides <*bi*convex> <*bi*serrate> **b** : coming or occurring two times <*bi*weekly> – often disapproved in this sense because of the likelihood of confusion with sense 1b; compare SEMI- **3** : between, involving, or affecting two (specified) symmetrical parts <*bi*aural> **4 a** : containing one (specified) constituent in double the proportion of the other constituent or in double the ordinary proportion <*bi*carbonate> **b** : DI- 2 <*bi*phenyl>

mon- *or* **mono-** \ *under stress the (1st) "o" is sometimes ō although not shown at individual entries* \ *comb form* [ME, fr. MF & L; MF, fr. LL, fr. Gk, fr. *monos* alone, single – more at MONK] **1** : one : single : alone <*mono*plane> <*mono*drama> <*mono*phobia> **2 a** : containing one (usu. specified) atom, radical, or group <*mono*hydrate> <*mono*oxide> **b** : monomolecular <*mono*film> <*mono*layer>

tri- *comb form* [ME, fr. L (fr. *tri-, tres*) & Gk, fr. *tri-, treis* – more at THREE] **1** : three <*tri*costate> having three elements or parts <*tri*graph> **2** : into three <*tri*sect> **3** : thrice <*tri*weekly> : every third <*tri*monthly>

B USING CONTEXT CLUES

Place an X in front of each correct answer. The word may be used correctly in one or both of the sentences.

1. The monologue lasted ten minutes means
   ___a. the conversation between the two people was very short.
   ___b. the speaker talked for ten minutes.

2. The monolith was dedicated to the memory of the early pioneers means
   ___a. the book was dedicated to the early pioneers.
   ___b. the monument honored the early pioneers.

3. Most Americans practice monogamy means
   ___a. most Americans have only one mate.
   ___b. most Americans have more than one mate.

4. The painting has a monochromatic color scheme means
   ___a. the artist used many colors.
   ___b. the artist used only one color.

5. The man had a biased opinion means
   ___a. he had a neutral and objective opinion.
   ___b. he favored one side too much.

Check your answers with the Key on page 137.

C CHECKING THE MEANING

Read the words in the boxes. Choose the word that best completes the sentence under them. Write that word on the line. Then complete the next sentence by placing an X in front of the correct answer.

1. biannual | monolith

The school held a dance on a ______________________ basis.
This sentence means
___a. a dance was held once every two weeks.
___b. a dance was held twice a year.
___c. a dance was held once every two months.

2. biannual | biennial

Some types of plants are ______________________.
This sentence means
___a. these plants will live for two years.
___b. these plants will live only one year.
___c. these plants will live only two months.

3. triarchy | monologue

The kingdom was ruled by a ______________________.
This sentence means
___a. the kingdom had three rulers.
___b. the kingdom had more than three rulers.
___c. the kingdom had only one ruler.

4. triarchy | triennial

The town held a fair on a ______________________ basis.
This sentence means
___a. the fair was held once every three weeks.
___b. the fair was held once every three months.
___c. the fair was held once every three years.

5. biannual | triangle

The ______________________ is a very common geometric figure.
This sentence means
___a. the geometric figure has three sides.
___b. the geometric figure has five sides.
___c. the geometric figure has six sides.

Check your answers with the Key on page 137.

D COMPLETING THE SENTENCES

Choose a word from the box that best completes each sentence. Write it on the line.

biased	triangle	monogamy	monologue
monolith	biannual	triarchy	monochromatic

1. People involved in debates are almost always ____________________.
2. The student was required to memorize a lengthy ________________ for the play.
3. The interior decorator chose a ____________________ color scheme.
4. The marble __________________ was extremely expensive.
5. Marriage to only one mate is called _______________________.

Check your answers with the Key on page 137.

E USING THE SKILL

Underline the word that best completes each sentence.

1. The country was governed by a (monolith, triarchy).
2. The student council election was held on a (biased, biannual) basis.
3. We visit Grandmother on a (biennial, triarchy) basis.
4. A (triennial, triangle) is a three-sided figure.
5. A (triangle, triennial) event occurs every three years.

Check your answers with the Key on page 137.

F SUPPLEMENTARY WRITING EXERCISE

The prefixes that were taught in this lesson are:

mono-	bi-	tri-

Write sentences in which you use each of the prefixes in a word in the sentence.

1. ____
2. ____
3. ____

A WRITING THE WORDS

A. Write these words on the blank lines.
Then say each word.

Write

quadrant	1.	______________
quadrennial	2.	______________
quadrilateral	3.	______________
quadruped	4.	______________
pentagon	5.	______________
pentarchy	6.	______________
pentathlon	7.	______________
hexagon	8.	______________
hexapod	9.	______________
hexameter	10.	______________

B. Each word begins with a prefix.
Write the prefix for each word.

1. ______________
2. ______________
3. ______________
4. ______________
5. ______________
6. ______________
7. ______________
8. ______________
9. ______________
10. ______________

THESE PREFIXES HAVE MEANINGS THAT RELATE TO **NUMBERS**.

SEQUENCE 9-2

hexa- *or* **hex-** *comb form* [Gk, fr. *hex* six – more at SIX] **1** : six <*hex*amerous> **2** : containing six atoms, groups, or equivalents <*hex*ane>

quadri- *or* **quadr-** or **quadru-** *comb form* [ME, fr. L; akin to L *quattuor* four] **1 a** : four <*quadri*lingual> <*quadru*mana> **b** : square <*quad*ric> **2** : fourth <*quadri*centennial>

penta- or **pent-** *comb form* [ME, fr. Gk, fr. *pente* – more at FIVE] **1** : five <*penta*hedron> **2** : containing five atoms, groups, or equivalents <*pent*ane>

B USING CONTEXT CLUES

Place an X in front of each correct answer. The word may be used correctly in one or both of the sentences.

1. The student drew a quadrant with his protractor means
   ___a. he drew one-quarter of a circle.
   ___b. he drew half of a circle.

2. The presidential election is a quadrennial event means
   ___a. the event happens every two years.
   ___b. the event happens every four years.

3. The shape is quadrilateral means
   ___a. it has three sides of equal length.
   ___b. it contains four sides and four angles.

4. A quadruped has
   ___a. four feet.
   ___b. three feet.

5. A building shaped like a pentagon must have
   ___a. five sides.
   ___b. more than five sides.

Check your answers with the Key on page 137.

C CHECKING THE MEANING

Read the words in the boxes. Choose the word that best completes the sentence under them. Write that word on the line. Then complete the next sentence by placing an X in front of the correct answer.

1. | hexapod | | pentarchy |

A __________________ is a rare form of government.
This sentence means
___a. a government with two leaders is rare.
___b. a government with no leaders is rare.
___c. a government with five leaders is rare.

2. | hexagon | | quadrant |

The fence formed a _________________________ when the yard was enclosed.
This sentence means
___a. the fence formed a figure with three sides.
___b. the fence formed a figure with six sides.
___c. the fence formed a square.

3. | pentarchy | | pentathlon |

The athlete set a new world record in the _______________________.
This sentence means
___a. the athlete participated in a wrestling event.
___b. the athlete participated in ten events.
___c. the athlete participated in five events.

4. | quadruped | | hexameter |

The poet used _________________ in many of his poems.
This sentence means
___a. the poet's poems consisted of six feet or measures per line.
___b. the poet wrote poems that did not rhyme.
___c. the poet wrote poems with five metrical feet per line.

5. | hexameter | | hexapod |

The insect is a _______________________.
This sentence means
___a. the insect has two heads.
___b. the insect has six legs.
___c. the insect has no eyes.

Check your answers with the Key on page 137.

SEQUENCE 9-2

D COMPLETING THE SENTENCES

Choose a word from the box that best completes each sentence. Write it on the line.

quadrant	pentagon	hexagon	quadrilateral
pentarchy	hexameter	quadruped	quadrennial

1. A horse is a type of ____________________.

2. The poem served as an example of ____________________.

3. The Soap Box Derby was a ____________________ event.

4. A ________________ is a geometric figure having five sides.

5. One __________________ of the circle graph represented money spent by the club.

Check your answers with the Key on page 137.

E USING THE SKILL

Underline the word that best completes each sentence.

1. A (hexagon, pentarchy) is a government ruled by five persons.

2. A geometric figure containing four angles is a (quadrant, quadrilateral).

3. A (hexapod, hexagon) is an animal with six legs.

4. An athletic contest with five events is a (pentarchy, pentathlon).

5. A (hexapod, pentagon) must have five sides and five angles.

Check your answers with the Key on page 137.

F SUPPLEMENTARY WRITING EXERCISE

The prefixes that were taught in this lesson are:

quadr- *or* quadri- *or* quadru-	pent-	hex-

Write sentences in which you use three of the prefixes in a word in the sentence.

1. ____

2. ____

3. ____

A WRITING THE WORDS

A. Write these words on the blank lines.
Then say each word.

	Write
September	1. ______________
septennial	2. ______________
septet	3. ______________
octagon	4. ______________
octopus	5. ______________
octet	6. ______________
octave	7. ______________
decimal	8. ______________
decimeter	9. ______________
decimate	10. ______________

B. Each word begins with a prefix.
Write the prefix for each word.

1. ______________
2. ______________
3. ______________
4. ______________
5. ______________
6. ______________
7. ______________
8. ______________
9. ______________
10. ______________

THESE PREFIXES HAVE MEANINGS THAT RELATE TO **NUMBERS**.

SEQUENCE 9-3

deci- *comb form* [F *déci-*, fr. L *decimus* tenth, fr. *decem* ten – more at TEN] : tenth part <*deci*normal>

octa- *or* **octo-** *also* **oct-** *comb form* [Gk *okta-*, *oktō-*, *okt-* (fr. *oktō*) & L *octo-*, *oct-*, fr. *octo* – more at EIGHT] : eight <*octa*merous> <*oct*ane> <*octo*roon>

sev-en \ ˈsev-ən \ *n* [ME, fr. *seven*, adj., fr. OE *seofon*; akin to OHG *sibun* seven, L *septem*, Gk *hepta*] **1** – see NUMBER table **2** : the seventh in a set or series <the ~ of diamonds> **3** : something having seven units or members

B USING CONTEXT CLUES

Place an X in front of each correct answer. The word may be used correctly in one or both of the sentences.

1. A septennial drought is one that
   ___a. does very little damage.
   ___b. lasts for seven years.

2. A septet is a musical composition
   ___a. written strictly for string instruments.
   ___b. for seven voices or seven instruments.

3. A stop sign is shaped like an octagon means
   ___a. the stop sign has eight sides.
   ___b. the stop sign has five sides.

4. An octopus
   ___a. has eight legs.
   ___b. must have more than eight legs.

5. An octet is formed by
   ___a. twenty or more professional musicians.
   ___b. eight voices or eight instruments.

Check your answers with the Key on page 137.

C CHECKING THE MEANING

Read the words in the boxes. Choose the word that best completes the sentence under them. Write that word on the line. Then complete the next sentence by placing an X in front of the correct answer.

1. octet | octave

The student recited a religious ______________________________ for her speech class.
This sentence means
___a. the student recited a religious passage from the Bible.
___b. the student recited a religious folk tale.
___c. the student recited eight lines of religious verse.

2. September | septet

In many places, school begins in ______________________________.
This sentence means
___a. school begins in the seventh month of the Roman calendar.
___b. school begins in the eleventh month of the year.
___c. school begins during the spring of the year.

3. decimeter | decimal

Metrics are based on the ______________________________ system of measurement.
This sentence means
___a. the system is based on increments of five.
___b. the system is based on increments of ten.
___c. the system is based on ancient Arabic measurement.

4. decimeter | octagon

A ______________________________ is a metric unit of measure.
This sentence means
___a. it is equal in length to ten miles.
___b. it represents two miles in length.
___c. it represents one tenth of a meter.

5. decimate | octet

A war will often ______________________________ a society.
This sentence means
___a. the entire society is destroyed.
___b. war often helps to preserve a society.
___c. one tenth of the society is destroyed.

Check your answers with the Key on page 137.

D COMPLETING THE SENTENCES

Choose a word from the box that best completes each sentence. Write it on the line.

septet	octet	octopus	September
octave	octagon	decimal	septennial

1. An ______________________ is a unit of musical measure.
2. An ______________________ is a sea mollusk with eight legs.
3. An ______________________ is an eight-sided geometric figure.
4. A ______________________ election is held once every seven years.
5. ______________________ is one of the twelve months of the year.

Check your answers with the Key on page 137.

E USING THE SKILL

Underline the word that best completes each sentence.

1. A (octet, septet) is a group of seven musicians.
2. A (decimate, decimal) system increases by tens.
3. One tenth of a meter is called a (decimeter, decimal).
4. The wrecking company was about to (octave, decimate) the building.
5. A composition written for an (octave, octet) requires eight instruments.

Check your answers with the Key on page 137.

F SUPPLEMENTARY WRITING EXERCISE

The prefixes that were taught in this lesson are:

sept-	oct-	deci-

Write sentences in which you use each of the prefixes in a word in the sentence.

1. ____
2. ____
3. ____

A WRITING THE WORDS

A. Write these words on the blank lines.
Then say each word.

Write

philanthropy	1.	________________
philanthropist	2.	________________
philatelist	3.	________________
polytheist	4.	________________
polygamous	5.	________________
misogyny	6.	________________
miscreant	7.	________________
misogamist	8.	________________
misanthropist	9.	________________
miscegenation	10.	________________

B. Each word begins with a prefix.
Write the prefix for each word.

1. ________________
2. ________________
3. ________________
4. ________________
5. ________________
6. ________________
7. ________________
8. ________________
9. ________________
10. ________________

THESE PREFIXES HAVE MEANINGS THAT CONCERN
MAN AND **HIS RELATIONSHIPS**.

SEQUENCE 9-4

[1]**mis-** *prefix* [partly fr. ME, fr. OE; partly fr. ME *mes-*, *mis-*, fr. OF *mes-*, of Gmc origin; akin to OE *mis-*; akin to OE *missan* to miss] **1 a** : badly : wrongly <*mis*judge> **b** : unfavorably <*mis*esteem> **c** : in a suspicious manner <*mis*doubt> **2** : bad : wrong <*mis*deed> **3** : opposite or lack of <*mis*trust> **4** : not <*mis*know>
[2]**mis-** *or* **miso-** *comb form* [Gk, fr. *misein* to hate] : hatred <*miso*gamy>

phil- *or* **philo-** *comb form* [ME, fr. OF, fr. L, fr. Gk, fr. *philos* dear, friendly] : loving : having an affinity for <*philo*progenitive>
[1]**phil-** \ fil \ *or* **-phile** \ fīl \ *n comb form* [F *-phile*, fr. Gk *-philos* or *-philous*] : lover : one having an affinity for or a strong attraction to <acido*phil*> <Slavo*phile*>

[2]**phil-** \" \ or **-phile** \" \ *adj comb form* [NL *-philus*, fr. L, fr. Gk *-philos*] : loving : having a fondness or affinity for <hemo*phile*> <Franco*phil*>

poly- *comb form* [ME, fr. L, fr. Gk, fr. *polys*; akin to OE *full* full] **1 a** : many : several : much : MULTI- <*poly*chotomous> <*poly*gyny> **b** : excessive : abnormal : HYPER- <*poly*phagia> **2 a** : containing an indefinite number of more than one of a (specified) substance <*poly*sulfide> **b** : polymeric : polymer of a (specified) monomer <*poly*ethylene> <*poly*adenylic acid>

B USING CONTEXT CLUES

Place an X in front of each correct answer. The word may be used correctly in one or both of the sentences.

1. A philanthropist is one who
   ___a. shows true concern and kindness for humanity.
   ___b. shows no concern for humanity.

2. A person who is involved in philanthropy is
   ___a. harmful to humanity.
   ___b. beneficial to humanity.

3. The man is a philatelist means
   ___a. he collects stamps.
   ___b. he collects baseball cards.

4. The man professed a true misogyny means
   ___a. he hated men.
   ___b. he hated women.

5. A hermit is often a misanthropist means
   ___a. a hermit trusts his fellow man.
   ___b. a hermit dislikes his fellow man.

Check your answers with the Key on page 138.

C CHECKING THE MEANING

Read the words in the boxes. Choose the word that best completes the sentence under them. Write that word on the line. Then complete the next sentence by placing an X in front of the correct answer.

1. polytheist | philanthropist

The leader of the cult is a ______________________________.
This sentence means
___a. he believes in more than one God.
___b. he believes there is one God.
___c. he does not believe in God.

2. philatelist | misogamist

The man was a devout ______________________________.
This sentence means
___a. he believed in marriage for all people.
___b. he hated marriage.
___c. he felt divorce was a sinful act.

3. miscreant | misogyny

The teenage boy became a ____________________________ at an early age.
This sentence means
___a. the boy acted with kindness.
___b. the boy was very brave.
___c. the boy became vicious.

4. misanthropist | miscegenation

The practice of ______________________________ is frowned upon by many.
This sentence means
___a. marriage between family members is frowned upon.
___b. interbreeding between races is not accepted by all.
___c. marriage between people of different ages is not right.

5. polygamous | misogyny

Many Middle East countries believe in ________________________ relationships.
This sentence means
___a. they believe in having more than one wife at the same time.
___b. they believe in permanent relationships.
___c. they do not believe in divorce.

Check your answers with the Key on page 138.

D COMPLETING THE SENTENCES

Choose a word from the box that best completes each sentence. Write it on the line.

philanthropist	philatelist	misanthropist	miscreant
miscegenation	philanthropy	misogyny	misogamist

1. The ____________________ donated money to help build a new orphanage.
2. Medical institutions are a useful ____________________.
3. After his divorce, the man became a ____________________.
4. To be a ____________________ is to be vicious.
5. The ____________________ had spent many years completing his collection.

Check your answers with the Key on page 138.

E USING THE SKILL

Underline the word that best completes each sentence.

1. Disappointed in his fellow man, the man became a (miscreant, misanthropist).
2. Racists frown upon (misogyny, miscegenation).
3. Hatred of women is called (misogyny, misogamist).
4. Organized religions often frown upon (miscreant, polytheist) ideas.
5. The law prohibits (philatelist, polygamous) relations in our society.

Check your answers with the Key on page 138.

F SUPPLEMENTARY WRITING EXERCISE

The prefixes that were taught in this lesson are:

phil- *or* philo- poly- mis-

Write sentences in which you use each of the prefixes in a word in the sentence.

1. ____________________
2. ____________________
3. ____________________

A WRITING THE WORDS

A. Write these words on the blank lines.
Then say each word.

	Write
apogee	1. ____________
apodal	2. ____________
apologue	3. ____________
microbe	4. ____________
micrometer	5. ____________
microcosm	6. ____________
microfilm	7. ____________
perimeter	8. ____________
periphery	9. ____________
perigee	10. ____________

B. Each word begins with a prefix.
Write the prefix for each word.

1. ____________
2. ____________
3. ____________
4. ____________
5. ____________
6. ____________
7. ____________
8. ____________
9. ____________
10. ____________

THESE PREFIXES HAVE MEANINGS THAT RELATE TO
SIZE, **DISTANCE**, OR **CONDITION**.

SEQUENCE 9-5

apo- *or* **ap-** *prefix* [ME, fr. MF & L; MF, fr. L, fr. Gk, fr. *apo* – more at OF] **1** : away from : off <*ap*helion> **2** : detached : separate <*apo*carpous> **3** : formed from : related to <*apo*morphine>

micr- *or* **micro-** *comb form* [ME *micro-*, fr. L, fr. Gk *mikr-*, *mikro-*, fr. *mikros*, *smikros* small, short; akin to OE *smēalic* careful, exquisite] **1 a** : small : minute <*micro*film> **b** : used for or involving minute quantities or variations <*micro*barograph> **c** : minutely <*micro*level> **2** : one millionth part of a (specified) unit <*micro*gram> <*micro*ohm> **3 a** : using microscopy <*micro*dissection> : used in microscopy **b** : revealed by or having the structure discernible only by microscopical examination <*micro*organism> **4** : abnormally small <*micro*cyte> **5** : of or relating to a small area <*micro*climate> **6** : employed in or connected with microphotographing or microfilming <*micro*copy>

peri- *prefix* [L, fr. Gk, around, in excess, fr. *peri*; akin to Gk *peran* to pass through – more at FARE] **1** : all around : about <*peri*scope> **2** : near <*peri*helion> **3** : enclosing : surrounding <*peri*neurium>

B USING CONTEXT CLUES

Place an X in front of each correct answer. The word may be used correctly in one or both of the sentences.

1. The apogee of the satellite's orbit was 18,000 miles means
   ___a. the lowest point of the orbit was 18,000 miles.
   ___b. the highest point of the orbit was 18,000 miles.

2. Alice planted flowers around the pool's perimeter means
   ___a. she planted flowers at the deep end of the pool.
   ___b. she planted flowers all around the pool.

3. A snake is an apodal creature means
   ___a. a snake is a cold-blooded animal.
   ___b. a snake has no legs.

4. The teacher asked the student to write an apologue means
   ___a. the student was asked to write a story with a moral.
   ___b. the student was asked to write a science fiction story.

5. A microbe was the cause of the disease means
   ___a. a tiny microscopic organism caused the disease.
   ___b. unsanitary living conditions caused the disease.

Check your answers with the Key on page 138.

C CHECKING THE MEANING

Read the words in the boxes. Choose the word that best completes the sentence under them. Write that word on the line. Then complete the next sentence by placing an X in front of the correct answer.

1. | micrometer | | microcosm |

The ______________________ on display in the museum was a popular exhibit.
This sentence means
___a. the model of the universe in miniature was a popular exhibit.
___b. the antique cars were a popular exhibit.
___c. the fossils on display were a popular exhibit.

2. | perimeter | | apologue |

The ______________________ of the square was 40 feet.
This sentence means
___a. the square was a very small square.
___b. the side of the square measured 40 feet.
___c. the distance around the square was 40 feet.

3. | periphery | | perigee |

The ______________________ of the prison yard was lined with barbed wire.
This sentence means
___a. the inner courtyard of the prison was lined with barbed wire.
___b. the main gate of the prison was made of barbed wire.
___c. the outer boundary of the prison was lined with barbed wire.

4. | perigee | | microcosm |

Astronomers are familiar with the ______________________ of each planet.
This sentence means
___a. astronomers are familiar with the orbit patterns of each planet.
___b. astronomers are familiar with the physical makeup of each planet.
___c. astronomers study all characteristics of each planet.

5. | apogee | | microfilm |

Important information is often stored on ______________________.
This sentence means
___a. information is often stored in special cameras.
___b. information is often stored in the form of small photographs.
___c. information is often stored in special machines.

Check your answers with the Key on page 138.

D COMPLETING THE SENTENCES

Choose a word from the box that best completes each sentence. Write it on the line.

apogee	microbe	microcosm	micrometer
apodal	apologue	microfilm	perimeter

1. A fish is an ____________________ form of life.
2. A ____________________ is often the cause of disease.
3. The ____________________ emphasized the quality of honesty.
4. A ____________________ is a delicate measuring instrument.
5. The ____________________ of the airplane's flight plan was 30,000 feet.

Check your answers with the Key on page 138.

E USING THE SKILL

Underline the word that best completes each sentence.

1. Storing large quantities of information is easy with (microbe, microfilm).
2. A (microcosm, apogee) makes examination of the universe less complicated.
3. The (apodal, perimeter) of the square was 360 inches.
4. The (periphery, microcosm) of the estate was lined with trees.
5. The (apologue, perigee) of the satellite was 500,000 miles from Earth.

Check your answers with the Key on page 138.

F SUPPLEMENTARY WRITING EXERCISE

The prefixes that were taught in this lesson are:

apo- *or* ap-	micro-	peri-

Write sentences in which you use each of the prefixes in a word in the sentence.

1. ____
2. ____
3. ____

A WRITING THE WORDS

A. Write these words on the blank lines.
Then say each word.

	Write
autograph	1. ______________________
autocrat	2. ______________________
autonomy	3. ______________________
sympathy	4. ______________________
symmetry	5. ______________________
symposium	6. ______________________
coerce	7. ______________________
cohere	8. ______________________
cogent	9. ______________________
coagulate	10. ______________________

B. Each word begins with a prefix.
Write the prefix for each word.

1. ______________________

2. ______________________

3. ______________________

4. ______________________

5. ______________________

6. ______________________

7. ______________________

8. ______________________

9. ______________________

10. ______________________

THESE PREFIXES HAVE MEANINGS RELATED TO
ACTIONS OR **CONDITIONS**.

SEQUENCE 9-6

aut- *or* **auto-** *comb form* [Gk, fr. *autos* same – more at EKE] **1** : self : same one <*aut*ism> <*auto*biography> **2** : automatic : self-acting : self-regulating <*auto*dyne>

co- *prefix* [ME, fr. L, fr. *com-*; akin to OE *ge-*, perfective and collective prefix, Gk *koinos* common] **1** : with : together : joint : jointly <*co*exist> <*co*heir> **2** : in or to the same degree <*co*extensive> **3 a** : one that is associated in an action with another : fellow : partner <*co*author> <*co*-worker> **b** : having a usu. lesser share in duty or responsibility : alternate : deputy <*co*pilot> **4** : of, relating to, or constituting the complement of an angle <*co*sine> <*co*declination>

syn- *or* **sym-** *prefix* [ME, fr. OF, fr. L, fr. Gk, fr. *syn* with, together with] **1** : with : along with : together <*syn*clinal> <*sym*petalous> **2** : at the same time <*syn*esthesia>

B USING CONTEXT CLUES

Place an X in front of each correct answer. The word may be used correctly in one or both of the sentences.

1. The butterfat in the milk tended to coagulate means
   ___a. the butterfat was dispersed in the milk.
   ___b. the butterfat clotted together.

2. When you coerce someone to do a job,
   ___a. you force them to do the job.
   ___b. you ask them to do the job.

3. To have sympathy for a person means you
   ___a. have no feelings for the person.
   ___b. have the same feelings as the person.

4. When you sign your autograph,
   ___a. you write your own name.
   ___b. you write your own name by yourself.

5. When a person has autonomy,
   ___a. he has freedom to guide his own life.
   ___b. he has no freedom to guide his own life.

Check your answers with the Key on page 138.

C CHECKING THE MEANING

Read the words in the boxes. Choose the word that best completes the sentence under them. Write that word on the line. Then complete the next sentence by placing an X in front of the correct answer.

1. cohere | cogent

The facts seemed ____________________ to the criminal case.
This sentence means
___a. the facts were not related to the case.
___b. the facts were related to the case.
___c. the facts helped establish guilt.

2. coerce | coagulate

The manager will ____________________ the employees to work harder.
This sentence means
___a. the manager will pay the employees to work harder.
___b. the manager will ask the employees to work harder.
___c. the manager will force the employees to work harder.

3. symmetry | symposium

They met at a ____________________ concerned with health issues.
This sentence means
___a. they felt the same about health issues.
___b. they met to discuss health issues.
___c. they met to change health laws.

4. autograph | autocrat

The man ruled his home and family as an ____________________.
This sentence means
___a. the man had little authority in his home.
___b. the man had some authority in his home.
___c. the man had absolute authority in his home.

5. autonomy | sympathy

The new position offers complete ____________________.
This sentence means
___a. the position allows no decision making.
___b. the position allows some decision making.
___c. the position allows one to make all the decisions.

Check your answers with the Key on page 138.

D COMPLETING THE SENTENCES

Choose a word from the box that best completes each sentence. Write it on the line.

coerce	cohere	sympathy	autocrat
cogent	symmetry	symposium	autonomy

1. The challenger should not ____________________ you into the fight.
2. Your information is ________________________ to the case.
3. The new glue will cause the pages to ____________________________ better.
4. The man ran his business with complete _________________________.
5. Complete _______________________ can be achieved by using straight lines.

Check your answers with the Key on page 138.

E USING THE SKILL

Underline the word that best completes each sentence.

1. The medication will cause the blood to (cogent, coagulate).
2. A paragraph tends to (coerce, cohere) together if written correctly.
3. Your (autograph, autocrat) may be famous someday.
4. To gain (sympathy, symmetry), look sad.
5. Your parents allow you some degree of (autocrat, autonomy).

Check your answers with the Key on page 138.

F SUPPLEMENTARY WRITING EXERCISE

The prefixes that were taught in this lesson are:

auto-	sym-	co-

Write sentences in which you use each of the prefixes in a word in the sentence.

1. ____
2. ____
3. ____

A WRITING THE WORDS

A. Write these words on the blank lines.
Then say each word.

		Write
disburse	1.	____________
dispense	2.	____________
discern	3.	____________
discretion	4.	____________
permeate	5.	____________
perpetuate	6.	____________
perennial	7.	____________
diagram	8.	____________
diagnose	9.	____________
dialogue	10.	____________

B Each word begins with a prefix.
Write the prefix for each word.

1. ____________
2. ____________
3. ____________
4. ____________
5. ____________
6. ____________
7. ____________
8. ____________
9. ____________
10. ____________

THESE PREFIXES HAVE MEANINGS RELATED TO **SEPARATION INTO PARTS** OR **MOVING THROUGH**.

SEQUENCE 9-7

dia- *also* **di-** *prefix* [ME, fr. OF, fr. L, fr. Gk, through, apart, fr. *dia*; akin to L *dis-*] through <*dia*positive> across <*dia*dromous>

dis- *prefix* [ME *dis-*, *des-*, fr. OF & L; OF *des-*, *dis-*, fr. L *dis-*, lit., apart; akin to OE *te-* apart, L *duo* two – more at TWO] **1 a** : do the opposite of <*dis*establish> **b** : deprive of (a specified quality, rank, or object) <*dis*able> <*dis*prince> <*dis*frock> **c** : exclude or expel from <*dis*bar> **2** : opposite or absence of <*dis*union> <*dis*affection> **3** : not <*dis*-agreeable> **4** : completely <*dis*annul> **5** : [by folk etymology] : DYS- <*dis*function>

per- *prefix* [L, through, throughout, thoroughly, to destruction, fr. *per*] **1** : throughout : thoroughly <*per*chlorinate> **2 a** : containing the largest possible or a relatively large proportion of a (specified) chemical element <*per*chloride> **b** : containing an element in its highest or a high oxidation state <*per*-chloric acid>

B USING CONTEXT CLUES

Place an X in front of each correct answer. The word may be used correctly in one or both of the sentences.

1. A diagram was used means
   ___a. a drawing to represent something was used.
   ___b. a drawing to reflect something was used.

2. To diagnose a disease is to
   ___a. recognize a disease by signs and symptoms.
   ___b. prescribe a treatment for a disease.

3. A dialogue is
   ___a. a conversation between two people.
   ___b. an argument between two people.

4. The government will disburse the funds means
   ___a. the government will collect funds.
   ___b. the government will give out funds.

5. A song that is a perennial favorite is
   ___a. a song that has lasted one year.
   ___b. a song that has lasted through the years.

Check your answers with the Key on page 139.

C CHECKING THE MEANING

Read the words in the boxes. Choose the word that best completes the sentence under them. Write that word on the line. Then complete the next sentence by placing an X in front of the correct answer.

1. perpetrate | permeate

The odor will ______________________________ the room.
This sentence means
___a. the odor will go away.
___b. the odor will get stronger.
___c. the odor will spread throughout the room.

2. dispense | discern

You must ________________________ between what is right and wrong.
This sentence means
___a. you must know and recognize right from wrong.
___b. you must become angry about what is wrong.
___c. you must become happy about what is right.

3. discretion | disburse

Use ______________________ when you make decisions.
This sentence means
___a. you must let luck help make decisions.
___b. you must make responsible decisions.
___c. you must disregard caution when making decisions.

4. perennial | disburse

The agency will _____________________ funds.
This sentence means
___a. the agency will collect money.
___b. the agency will bank money.
___c. the agency will give out money.

5. diagram | diagnose

The technician will _____________________ the problem.
This sentence means
___a. the technician will determine the problem.
___b. the technician will solve the problem.
___c. the technician will ignore the problem.

Check your answers with the Key on page 139.

D COMPLETING THE SENTENCES

Choose a word from the box that best completes each sentence. Write it on the line.

dialogue	dispense	diagram	permeate
discern	discretion	diagnose	perennial

1. The doctor will ____________________ the child's ailment.

2. A wise judge can often ____________________ the truth.

3. Use ____________________ when selecting your friends.

4. The flu that comes in winter is ____________________.

5. The Red Cross will ____________________ emergency rations.

Check your answers with the Key on page 139.

E USING THE SKILL

Underline the word that best completes each sentence.

1. The teacher used a (diagram, discretion) to explain the difficult problem.

2. The odor will (discern, permeate) the building quickly.

3. The machine will (diagnose, dispense) the candy.

4. A (diagram, dialogue) is a two-way conversation.

5. The witness will (permeate, perpetrate) an injustice by lying.

Check your answers with the Key on page 139.

F SUPPLEMENTARY WRITING EXERCISE

The prefixes that were taught in this lesson are:

dis-	per-	dia-

Write sentences in which you use each of the prefixes in a word in the sentence.

1. ____

2. ____

3. ____

A WRITING THE WORDS

A. Write these words on the blank lines.
Then say each word.

Write

abridge	1.	______________
abdicate	2.	______________
abrogate	3.	______________
abolition	4.	______________
adjacent	5.	______________
adjunct	6.	______________
adamant	7.	______________
obese	8.	______________
obsolete	9.	______________
obliterate	10.	______________

B. Each word begins with a prefix.
Write the prefix for each word.

1. ______________
2. ______________
3. ______________
4. ______________
5. ______________
6. ______________
7. ______________
8. ______________
9. ______________
10. ______________

THESE PREFIXES HAVE MEANINGS RELATED TO **MOVEMENT** OR **DIRECTION**.

SEQUENCE 9-8

ab- *prefix* [ME, fr. OF & L; OF, fr. L *ab-*, *abs-*, *a-*, fr. *ab, a* – more at OF] : from : away : off <*ab*axial> <*ab*strict>

ad- *or* **ac-** *or* **af-** *or* **ag-** *or* **al-** *or* **ap-** *or* **as-** *or* **at-** *prefix* [ME, fr. MF, OF & L; MF, fr. OF, fr. L, fr. *ad* – more at AT] **1** : to : toward – usu. *ac-* before *c, k*, or *q* <*ac*culturation> and *af-* before *f* and *ag-* before *g* <*ag*grade> and *al-* before *l* <*al*literation> and *ap-* before *p* <*ap*proximal> and *as-* before *s* <*as*suasive> and *at-* before *t* <*at*tune> and *ad-* before other sounds but sometimes *ad-* even before one of the listed consonants <*ad*sorb> **2** : near: adjacent to – in this sense always in the form *ad-* <*ad*renal>

ob- *prefix* [NL, fr. L, in the way, against, toward, fr. *ob* in the way of, on account of – more at EPI-] : inversely <*ob*ovate>

B USING CONTEXT CLUES

Place an X in front of each correct answer. The word may be used correctly in one or both of the sentences.

1. He remained adamant about his decision means
   ___a. he would change his decision.
   ___b. he would not change his decision.

2. The land was adjacent to a lake means
   ___a. the land was far from a lake.
   ___b. the land was very near a lake.

3. The king will abdicate his throne means
   ___a. the king will stay on his throne.
   ___b. the king will give up his throne.

4. The new president will abrogate the old law means
   ___a. the president will support the old law.
   ___b. the president will abolish the old law.

5. The gas will obliterate all signs of life means
   ___a. the gas will destroy all traces of life.
   ___b. the gas will reveal all traces of life.

Check your answers with the Key on page 139.

C CHECKING THE MEANING

Read the words in the boxes. Choose the word that best completes the sentence under them. Write that word on the line. Then complete the next sentence by placing an X in front of the correct answer.

1. obese | obsolete

The dangerous pesticide is now ______________________.
This sentence means
___a. the dangerous pesticide is used a great deal.
___b. the dangerous pesticide can only be used once.
___c. the dangerous pesticide is no longer available for use.

2. abridge | abrogate

The book-publishing company will ____________________ the lengthy novel.
This sentence means
___a. the company will publish the lengthy novel.
___b. the company will condense the lengthy novel.
___c. the company will not publish the novel.

3. abdicate | abolition

Many people believe in the ______________________ of a monarchy.
This sentence means
___a. many people believe in supporting a monarchy.
___b. many people believe in challenging a monarchy.
___c. many people believe in the elimination of a monarchy.

4. adjunct | adamant

The study of grammar is a necessary __________________ to the study of English.
This sentence means
___a. grammar is a necessary addition to the study of English.
___b. grammar is not related to the study of English.
___c. grammar has no reason for being studied.

5. adjacent | obliterate

The criminal will ________________________ his trail through the woods.
This sentence means
___a. the criminal will establish his trail.
___b. the criminal will destroy all signs of his trail.
___c. the criminal will make his trail through the woods.

Check your answers with the Key on page 139.

D COMPLETING THE SENTENCES

Choose a word from the box that best completes each sentence. Write it on the line.

obese	adjacent	abdicate	abrogate
obsolete	adjunct	abolition	abridge

1. New plastics may one day make glass ______________________.
2. Our home is ____________________ to the city park.
3. The man ate heavily and became __________________________.
4. We hope to ________________________ all old laws that are ineffective.
5. A student may wish to ______________________ his many pages of notes.

Check your answers with the Key on page 139.

E USING THE SKILL

Underline the word that best completes each sentence.

1. The judge remained (adjunct, adamant) about his decision.
2. The king may (abolition, abdicate) his throne.
3. The new Congress will (abridge, abrogate) many unsettled issues.
4. The emerging sunshine helped (obsolete, obliterate) all traces of dampness.
5. The new city hall is an (adjacent, adjunct) to the courthouse.

Check your answers with the Key on page 139.

F SUPPLEMENTARY WRITING EXERCISE

The prefixes that were taught in this lesson are:

ab-	ad-	ob-

Write sentences in which you use each of the prefixes in a word in the sentence.

1. ____
2. ____
3. ____

A WRITING THE WORDS

A. Write these words on the blank lines.
Then say each word.

		Write
expiate	1.	______________
excerpt	2.	______________
expedient	3.	______________
expatriate	4.	______________
subordinate	5.	______________
subterfuge	6.	______________
subjugate	7.	______________
deduce	8.	______________
delineate	9.	______________
dehydration	10.	______________

B. Each word begins with a prefix.
Write the prefix for each word.

1. ______________
2. ______________
3. ______________
4. ______________
5. ______________
6. ______________
7. ______________
8. ______________
9. ______________
10. ______________

THESE PREFIXES HAVE MEANINGS THAT **GIVE POSITION**.

SEQUENCE 9-9

de- *prefix* [ME, fr. OF *de-*, *des-*, partly fr. L *de-* from, down, away (fr. *de*) and partly fr. L *dis-*; L *de* akin to OIr *di* from, OE *tō* to – more at TO, DIS-] **1 a** : do the opposite of <*de*vitalize> <*de*activate> **b** : reverse of <*de*-emphasis> **2 a** : remove (a specified thing) from <*de*louse> <*de*hydrogenate> **b** : remove from (a specified thing) <*de*throne> **3** : reduce <*de*value> **4** : something derived from (a specified thing) <*de*compound> : derived from something (of a specified nature) <*de*nominative> **5** : get off of (a specified thing) <*de*train> **6** : having a molecule characterized by the removal of one or more atoms (of a specified element) <*de*oxy->

ex- \ *e also occurs in this prefix where only* i *is shown below (as in "express") and* ks *sometimes occurs where only* gz *is shown (as in "exact")* \ *prefix* [ME, fr. OF & L; OF, fr. L (also, intensive prefix), fr. *ex* out of, from; akin to Gk *ex, ex-* out of, from, OSlav *iz*] **1** : out of : outside <*ex*clave> **2** : not <*ex*stipulate> **3** : \(ˌ)eks, ˈeks \ [ME, fr. LL, fr. L] former : <*ex*-president> <*ex*-child actor>

sub- *prefix* [ME, fr. L, under, below, secretly, from below, up, near, fr. *sub* under, close to – more at UP] **1** : under : beneath : below <*sub*soil> <*sub*aqueous> **2 a** : subordinate : secondary : next lower than or inferior to <*sub*station> <*sub*editor> **b** : subordinate portion of : subdivision of <*sub*committee> <*sub*species> **c** : with repetition (as of a process) so as to form, stress, or deal with subordinate parts or relations <*sub*let> <*sub*contract> **3 a** : less than completely, perfectly, or normally : somewhat <*sub*dominant> <*sub*ovate> **b** (1) : containing less than the usual or normal amount of (such) an element or radical <*sub*oxide> (2) : basic – in names of salts <*sub*acetate> **4 a** : almost : nearly <*sub*erect> **b** : falling nearly in the category of and often adjoining : bordering upon <*sub*arctic>

B USING CONTEXT CLUES

Place an X in front of each correct answer. The word may be used correctly in one or both of the sentences.

1. A good detective will <u>deduce</u> a solution means
   ___a. a good detective can determine a solution from facts.
   ___b. a good detective can trace facts to a solution.

2. An explorer must carefully <u>delineate</u> his course means
   ___a. an explorer must plan his exact course.
   ___b. an explorer must have a detailed plan.

3. The soldier became an <u>expatriate</u> means
   ___a. the soldier came home to stay.
   ___b. the soldier gave up his native country.

4. A <u>confession</u> to your parents will expiate you means
   ___a. a confession will make amends to your parents.
   ___b. a confession will cause you to be punished.

5. The autocrat will <u>subjugate</u> you to his wishes means
   ___a. the autocrat will force you to submit to his wishes.
   ___b. the autocrat will allow you freedom.

Check your answers with the Key on page 139.

C CHECKING THE MEANING

Read the words in the boxes. Choose the word that best completes the sentence under them. Write that word on the line. Then complete the next sentence by placing an X in front of the correct answer.

1. | dehydration | | delineate |

To produce dried food, a process of ____________________ is necessary.
This sentence means
___a. moisture is added to food to make it dry.
___b. moisture is removed from food to make it dry.
___c. moisture is left in food to make it dry.

2. | excerpt | | expedient |

An ________________ from the book was used in the publisher's advertising plan.
This sentence means
___a. a selection was taken from the book.
___b. a selection was added to the book.
___c. only the book's cover was used for advertising.

3. | deduce | | expatriate |

A scientist may ________________________ a theory based on facts.
This sentence means
___a. facts lead a scientist away from a theory.
___b. facts may lead a scientist to a theory.
___c. a scientist may prove a theory.

4. | subterfuge | | subordinate |

Some people use ______________________ to conceal true feelings.
This sentence means
___a. some people will deceive others to conceal true feelings.
___b. some people will terrorize others to conceal true feelings.
___c. some people will bewilder others to conceal true feelings.

5. | subjugate | | expiate |

Wise parents will not ____________________ their children.
This sentence means
___a. wise parents will not be too easy with their children.
___b. wise parents will not be too friendly with their children.
___c. wise parents will not force their children to submit to their will.

Check your answers with the Key on page 139.

D COMPLETING THE SENTENCES

Choose a word from the box that best completes each sentence. Write it on the line.

subjugate	expiate	delineate	excerpt
subordinate	expedient	dehydration	subterfuge

1. A ______________________ clause contains a subject and a verb.

2. The most ______________________ way to the office is via the elevator.

3. The writer was careful to ___________________ each character in his book.

4. The "little white lie" is a form of ___________________________.

5. Too much exposure to the sun can cause _______________________ in one's body

Check your answers with the Key on page 139.

E USING THE SKILL

Underline the word that best completes each sentence.

1. The physicist will try to (deduce, excerpt) a solution to the energy problem.

2. An (expedient, expatriate) can lose his citizenship.

3. A criminal may use (subjugate, subterfuge) to escape prison.

4. The General will (deduce, delineate) his war plans to his men.

5. An (expiate, excerpt) was taken from the poem and read over the microphone.

Check your answers with the Key on page 139.

F SUPPLEMENTARY WRITING EXERCISE

The prefixes that were taught in this lesson are:

ex-	sub-	de-

Write sentences in which you use each of the prefixes in a word in the sentence.

1. ____

2. ____

3. ____

A WRITING THE WORDS

A. Write these words on the blank lines.
Then say each word.

Write

synopsis	1.	____________
syndicate	2.	____________
synchronize	3.	____________
compassion	4.	____________
commune	5.	____________
communism	6.	____________
commensurate	7.	____________
concede	8.	____________
condone	9.	____________
conciliate	10.	____________

B. Each word begins with a prefix.
Write the prefix for each word.

1. ____________
2. ____________
3. ____________
4. ____________
5. ____________
6. ____________
7. ____________
8. ____________
9. ____________
10. ____________

THESE PREFIXES HAVE MEANINGS THAT MEAN **WITH** OR **TOGETHER**.

com- *or* **col-** *or* **con-** *prefix* [ME, fr. OF, fr. L, with, together, thoroughly – more at CO-] : with : together : jointly - usu. *com-* before *b, p,* or *m* <*com*ingle>, *col-* before *l* <*co*linear>, and *con-* before other sounds <*con*centrate>

syn- *or* **sym-** *prefix* [ME, fr. OF, fr. L, fr. Gk, fr. *syn* with, together with] **1** : with : along with : together <*syn*clinal> <*sym*petalous> **2** : at the same time <*syn*esthesia>

B USING CONTEXT CLUES

Place an X in front of each correct answer. The word may be used correctly in one or both of the sentences.

1. The swimming team will synchronize its movements means
 ___a. the swimmers will make different movements.
 ___b. the swimmers will make the same movement at the same time.

2. The newspaper will syndicate its news means
 ___a. the newspaper company will keep its own news.
 ___b. the newspaper will share its news with other people.

3. When you show compassion,
 ___a. you suffer with another.
 ___b. you bear the burden that another bears.

4. The candidate will concede the election means
 ___a. the candidate will win the election.
 ___b. the candidate will admit he lost the election.

5. Most people do not condone polygamy means
 ___a. most people support the practice of polygamy.
 ___b. most people will not overlook the practice of polygamy.

Check your answers with the Key on page 140.

C CHECKING THE MEANING

Read the words in the boxes. Choose the word that best completes the sentence under them. Write that word on the line. Then complete the next sentence by placing an X in front of the correct answer.

1. synchronize | synopsis

The student will write a ______________________________ of the story.
This sentence means
___a. the student will embellish the story.
___b. the student will rewrite the story.
___c. the student will condense the story.

2. commensurate | commune

The man desires to ____ with me.
This sentence means
___a. the man desires to live with me.
___b. the man desires to talk with me.
___c. the man desires to work with me.

3. communism | compassion

The practice of ______________________________ eliminates free enterprise.
This sentence means
___a. belief in equal distribution of goods eliminates free enterprise.
___b. belief in equality of the sexes eliminates free enterprise.
___c. belief in sharing responsibility eliminates free enterprise.

4. concede | condone

Most parents will not __________________________ a child that lies.
This sentence means
___a. parents are proud of a child that lies.
___b. parents will abandon a child that lies.
___c. parents will not excuse a child that lies.

5. syndicate | conciliate

They will _________________________ their differences at the meeting.
This sentence means
___a. they will argue over their differences.
___b. they will never agree on their differences.
___c. they will come to an agreement about their differences.

Check your answers with the Key on page 140.

D COMPLETING THE SENTENCES

Choose a word from the box that best completes each sentence. Write it on the line.

condone	synopsis	syndicate	commensurate
concede	conciliate	synchronize	compassion

1. Your salary will be ____________________ with your ability and experience.

2. To ____________________ in an argument is to lose the argument.

3. The arbitrator tried to ____________________ a peace between the two countries.

4. Most companies try to ____________________ all clocks in their buildings.

5. The law will not ____________________ lawbreakers.

Check your answers with the Key on page 140.

E USING THE SKILL

Underline the word that best completes each sentence.

1. The strobe light will (syndicate, synchronize) with the music.

2. The man wanted to (commensurate, commune) with his neighbor.

3. Most young people show (conciliate, compassion) for the elderly.

4. The teacher will not (concede, condone) poor conduct.

5. The book's (communism, synopsis) will familiarize you with the story.

Check your answers with the Key on page 140.

F SUPPLEMENTARY WRITING EXERCISE

The prefixes that were taught in this lesson are:

syn-	com-	con-

Write the sentences in which you use each of the prefixes in a word in the sentence.

1. ____

2. ____

3. ____

A WRITING THE WORDS

A. Write these words on the blank lines.
Then say each word.

Write

binocular	1.	________________
oculist	2.	________________
monocle	3.	________________
optic	4.	________________
optician	5.	________________
spectacle	6.	________________
spectator	7.	________________
specter	8.	________________
inspect	9.	________________
circumspect	10.	________________

B. Each word contains a word root or word stem. Write the word root or the word stem for each word.

1. ________________
2. ________________
3. ________________
4. ________________
5. ________________
6. ________________
7. ________________
8. ________________
9. ________________
10. ________________

THESE ROOTS HAVE MEANINGS RELATED TO **SIGHT** OR **SEEING**.

ocul- *or* **oculo-** *comb form* [L *ocul-*, fr. *oculus* – more at EYE] **1** : eye <*oculo*motor> **2** : ocular and <*oculo*cardiac>

op-tic \ ˈäp-tik \ *adj* [MF *optique*, fr. ML *opticus*, fr. Gk. *optikos*, fr. *opsesthai* to be going to see; akin to Gk *opsis* appearance, *ōps* eye – more at EYE] **1** : of or relating to vision or the eye **2** : dependent chiefly on vision for orientation

spec-ta-cle \ ˈspek-ti-kəl; *most often for 2, 3* - ˌ*tik-əl* \ *n* [ME, fr. MF, fr. L *spectaculum*, fr. *spectare* to watch, fr. *spectus*, pp. of *specere* to look, look at – more at SPY] **1 a** : something exhibited to view as unusual, notable, or entertaining; *esp* : an eye-catching or dramatic public display **b** : an object of curiosity or contempt <made a ~ of herself> **2** *pl* : EYEGLASSES **3** : something (as natural markings on an animal) suggesting a pair of glasses

B USING CONTEXT CLUES

Place an X in front of each correct answer. The word may be used correctly in one or both of the sentences.

1. The fireworks were a spectacle for all to see means
   ___a. the fireworks were a display for the public.
   ___b. the fireworks were very expensive.

2. Each spectator was charged admission to the game means
   ___a. people playing in the game paid an admission fee.
   ___b. people watching the game paid an admission fee.

3. The little boy thought he saw a specter means
   ___a. the boy thought he saw a ghost.
   ___b. the boy thought he saw an old friend.

4. The company asked the foreman to inspect the machinery means
   ___a. the foreman was asked to repair the machinery.
   ___b. the foreman was asked to examine the machinery.

5. The man was circumspect at all times means
   ___a. the man was always careless.
   ___b. the man was always cautious.

Check your answers with the Key on page 140.

C CHECKING THE MEANING

Read the words in the boxes. Choose the word that best completes the sentence under them. Write that word on the line. Then complete the next sentence by placing an X in front of the correct answer.

1. circumspect binocular

Human beings have ________________________ vision.
This sentence means
___a. they use both eyes to see.
___b. their eyes grow weak as they grow older.
___c. they need their eyes to survive.

2. oculist spectacle

The mother made her children appointments with an ____________________.
This sentence means
___a. the children will have their eyes examined.
___b. the children will have their ears examined.
___c. the children will have their teeth examined.

3. specter optician

The boy planned to be an ____________________ when he grew up.
This sentence means
___a. he would care for sick animals.
___b. he would study to be a magician.
___c. he would make and sell eyeglasses.

4. optic inspect

The lady suffers from severe ____________________ problems.
This sentence means
___a. she has a weak heart.
___b. she has a poor sense of hearing.
___c. she has trouble with her sense of sight.

5. monocle spectator

The prime minister wore a ____________________ whenever he was in public.
This sentence means
___a. he wore an eyeglass over one eye.
___b. he wore an official uniform.
___c. he wore a sword as a symbol of authority.

Check your answers with the Key on page 140.

D COMPLETING THE SENTENCES

Choose a word from the box that best completes each sentence. Write it on the line.

spectacle	specter	optician	circumspect
optic	oculist	inspect	spectator

1. The first moon landing was a ____________________ witnessed around the world.
2. The ______________________ nerve is responsible for the sense of sight.
3. Everyone in town thought a ___________________ lived in the haunted house.
4. The foreman will ____________________ the building site for unsafe conditions.
5. The ________________________ filled the prescription for eyeglasses.

Check your answers with the Key on page 140.

E USING THE SKILL

Underline the word that best completes each sentence.

1. A (binocular, monocle) improves vision in only one eye.
2. The (optic, oculist) examined the man's eyes.
3. Vision that is (binocular, circumspect) provides us with depth perception.
4. The (spectator, inspector) was late for the game's kickoff.
5. The lawyer approached each case with a (optic, circumspect) attitude.

Check your answers with the Key on page 140.

F SUPPLEMENTARY WRITING EXERCISE

The roots that were taught in this lesson are:

ocul- *or* oculo-	opt-	spect-

Write sentences in which you use each of the roots in a word in the sentence.

1. ____
2. ____
3. ____

A WRITING THE WORDS

A. Write these words on the blank lines. Then say each word.

Write

amicable	1.	____________
amiable	2.	____________
amorous	3.	____________
amatory	4.	____________
animate	5.	____________
animosity	6.	____________
unanimous	7.	____________
benefit	8.	____________
benevolent	9.	____________
benediction	10.	____________

B. Each word contains a word root or word stem. Write the word root or the word stem for each word.

1. ____________
2. ____________
3. ____________
4. ____________
5. ____________
6. ____________
7. ____________
8. ____________
9. ____________
10. ____________

THESE ROOTS HAVE MEANINGS RELATED TO **A STATE** OR A **CONDITION.**

SEQUENCE 9-12

ami-a-ble \ ˈā-mē-ə-bəl \ *adj* [ME, fr. MF, fr. LL *amicabilis* friendly, fr. L *amices* friend; akin to L *amare* to love] **1** *archaic* : PLEASING, ADMIRABLE **2 a** : generally agreeable <an ~ musical comedy> **b** : having a friendly, sociable, and congenial disposition – **ami-a-bil-i-ty** \ ˌā-mē-ə-ˈbil-ət-ē \ *n* - **ami-a-ble-ness** \ ˈā-mē-ə-bəl-nəs \ *n* - **ami-a-bly** \ -blē \ *adv*

an-i-mate \ ˈan-ə-mət \ *adj* [ME, fr. L *animatus*, pp. of *animare* to give life to, fr. *anima* breath, soul; akin to OE *ōthian* to breathe, L *animus* spirit, mind, courage, Gk *anemos* wind] **1 a** : possessing life : ALIVE **b** : of the kind or class of which life is a characteristic <all ~ creation> **2** : of or relating to animal life as opposed to plant life **3** : full of life : ANIMATED ***syn*** see LIVING ***ant*** inanimate – **an-i-mate-ly** *adv* – **an-i-mate-ness** *n*

bene-dic-tion \ ˌben-ə-ˈdik-shən \ *n* [ME *benediccioun*, fr. LL *benediction-, benedicto*, fr. *benedictus*, pp. of *benedicere* to bless, fr. L, to speak well of, fr. *bene* well + *dicere* to say – more at BOUNTY, DICTION] **1** : an expression of good wishes **2** : the invocation of a blessing; *esp* : the short blessing with which public worship is concluded **3** : *often cap* : a Roman Catholic or Anglo-Catholic devotion including the exposition of the eucharistic Host in the monstrance and the blessing of the people with it **4** : something that promotes goodness or well-being

B USING CONTEXT CLUES

Place an X in front of each correct answer. The word may be used correctly in one or both of the sentences.

1. The argument was settled in an <u>amicable</u> way means
   ___a. many harsh words were used.
   ___b. it was settled in a peaceful way.

2. He was <u>amiable</u> means
   ___a. he was not friendly.
   ___b. he was friendly.

3. The two people had an <u>amorous</u> relationship means
   ___a. they were deeply in love.
   ___b. they were constantly arguing.

4. The play had an <u>amatory</u> theme means
   ___a. the play dealt with love.
   ___b. the play dealt with death.

5. The professor wished to <u>animate</u> the lecture means
   ___a. he wished to make it more lively and interesting.
   ___b. he wished to make it more technical.

Check your answers with the Key on page 140.

C CHECKING THE MEANING

Read the words in the boxes. Choose the word that best completes the sentence under them. Write that word on the line. Then complete the next sentence by placing an X in front of the correct answer.

1. | animosity | | amorous |

The ______________________ the brothers felt for one another was felt by all.
This sentence means
___a. their love for one another was felt by all.
___b. the brothers had a great deal of affection for one another.
___c. the brothers had a great deal of dislike for one another.

2. | unanimous | | amiable |

The political party reached a __________________________ decision.
This sentence means
___a. everyone present agreed with the decision.
___b. no one agreed with the decision.
___c. only a fraction of the party agreed with the decision.

3. | amatory | | benevolent |

His offer to donate to the orphanage was a ______________________ offer.
This sentence means
___a. his offer was a kindly one.
___b. his offer was a foolish one.
___c. his offer was a charitable one.

4. | amicable | | benefit |

Good food and exercise are a ______________________ to one's health.
This sentence means
___a. good food and exercise are not important.
___b. good food and exercise have no affect on one's health.
___c. good food and exercise are good for one's health.

5. | benediction | | amiable |

The preacher asked a church member to give a ________________________.
This sentence means
___a. he asked the church member to direct the singing.
___b. he asked the church member to close with a blessing.
___c. he asked the church member to give the sermon.

Check your answers with the Key on page 140.

D COMPLETING THE SENTENCES

Choose a word from the box that best completes each sentence. Write it on the line.

amicable	amorous	animate	unanimous
amiable	amatory	animosity	benevolent

1. The organization was a __________________ one and did many good works.
2. The salesclerk was a very __________________ person.
3. The man felt his daughter was too young for an __________________ relationship.
4. The decision was a ______________________ one, with everyone casting a ballot.
5. The two independent nations had an __________________________ relationship.

Check your answers with the Key on page 140.

E USING THE SKILL

Underline the word that best completes each sentence.

1. The teenage girl liked to read books with an (amatory, animate) theme.
2. There was great (amorous, animosity) between the warring nations.
3. A (benefit, benevolent) was held to raise money for the charity.
4. The minister was well known for his use of a lengthy (animate, benediction).
5. The teacher hoped to (animate, animosity) her class lecture with puppets.

Check your answers with the Key on page 140.

F SUPPLEMENTARY WRITING EXERCISE

The roots that were taught in this lesson are:

am-	anim-	bene-

Write sentences in which you use each of the roots in a word in the sentence.

1. ____
2. ____
3. ____

A WRITING THE WORDS

A. Write these words on the blank lines.
Then say each word.

	Write
coincidence	1. ______________
accident	2. ______________
incident	3. ______________
capable	4. ______________
captivate	5. ______________
capture	6. ______________
capacious	7. ______________
credible	8. ______________
credentials	9. ______________
credence	10. ______________

B. Each word contains a word root or word stem.
Write the word root or the word stem for each word.

1. ______________
2. ______________
3. ______________
4. ______________
5. ______________
6. ______________
7. ______________
8. ______________
9. ______________
10. ______________

THESE ROOTS HAVE MEANINGS RELATED TO AN **ACTION**.

SEQUENCE 9-13

ca-pa-ble \ ˈkā-pə-bəl \ adj [MF or LL; MF capable, fr. LL *capabilis*, irreg. fr. L *capere* to take – more at HEAVE] **1** : SUSCEPTIBLE <a remark ~ of being misunderstood> **2** *obs* : COMPREHENSIVE **3** : having attributes (as physical or mental power) required for performance or accomplishment <a man ~ of intense concentration> **4** : having traits conducive to or admitting of <this woman is ~ of murder by violence – Robert Graves> **5** : having general efficiency and ability **6** : *obs* : having legal right to own, enjoy, or perform ***syn*** see ABLE ***ant*** incapable – **ca-pa-ble-ness** \ ˈkā-pə-bəl-nəs \ *n* – **ca-pa-bly** \ -pə-blē \ *adv*

cred-i-ble \ ˈkred-ə-bəl \ *adj* [ME, fr. L *credibilis*, fr. *credere*] : offering reasonable grounds for being believed <a ~ account of an accident> <a ~ witness> ***syn*** see PLAUSIBLE ***ant*** incredible

in-ci-dent \ ˈin(t)-səd-ənt, -sə- ˌdent \ *n* [ME, fr. MF, fr. ML *incident-, incidens*, fr. L, prp of *incedere* to fall into, fr. *in-* + *cadere* to fall – more at CHANCE] **1 a** : an occurrence of an action or situation that is a separate unit of experience : HAPPENING **b** : an accompanying minor occurrence or condition : CONCOMITANT **2** : an action likely to lead to grave consequences esp. in matters diplomatic <a serious border ~ > **3** : something dependent on or subordinate to something else of greater or principal importance

B USING CONTEXT CLUES

Place an X in front of each correct answer. The word may be used correctly in one or both of the sentences.

1. He ran into his old friend by <u>accident</u> means
 ___a. the meeting was arranged ahead of time.
 ___b. the meeting was not planned.

2. The newspaper reporter was asked to cover the <u>incident</u> means
 ___a. he was asked to report on a specific event.
 ___b. he was asked to write a movie review.

3. She was a <u>capable</u> seamstress means
 ___a. she was very skillful and competent.
 ___b. she was not a very good seamstress.

4. The girl's beauty would <u>captivate</u> all those who met her means
 ___a. the girl's beauty attracted little attention.
 ___b. the girl's beauty would charm everyone she met.

5. The boys tried to <u>capture</u> the wild rabbit means
 ___a. the boys tried to catch the rabbit.
 ___b. the boys tried to set the rabbit free.

Check your answers with the Key on page 141.

C CHECKING THE MEANING

Read the words in the boxes. Choose the word that best completes the sentence under them. Write that word on the line. Then complete the next sentence by placing an X in front of the correct answer.

1. credible   capable

The evidence produced by the lawyer was not ______________________.
This sentence means
___a. the evidence was not conclusive.
___b. the evidence was poor in quality.
___c. the evidence was not reliable.

2. credentials   credence

The newly hired maid presented her ______________________ to her employer.
This sentence means
___a. she presented her employer with a list of demands.
___b. she gave references to her employer.
___c. she asked her employer for specific days off.

3. capacious   capable

The rooms in the elaborate hotel were very ______________________.
This sentence means
___a. the rooms were very large.
___b. the rooms were furnished with antiques.
___c. the rooms were very expensive.

4. credence   incident

The scientist gave little ____________________ to the results of the experiment.
This sentence means
___a. the results were very accurate.
___b. the results were valid.
___c. the scientist had little faith in the results.

5. coincidence   capture

The fact that the friends bought identical dresses was a ____________________.
This sentence means
___a. they had planned to buy dresses that were identical.
___b. they had not planned to buy identical dresses.
___c. they were angry that their dresses were identical.

Check your answers with the Key on page 141.

D COMPLETING THE SENTENCES

Choose a word from the box that best completes each sentence. Write it on the line.

accident	incident	capable	coincidence
capture	captivate	capacious	credence

1. The meeting of the two college roommates was a ______________________.
2. Poor driving conditions were the cause of the ______________________.
3. Zoo attendants tried to ______________________ the injured lion.
4. He was a very ______________________ physician.
5. The actress used her acting abilities to ____________________ the audience.

Check your answers with the Key on page 141.

E USING THE SKILL

Underline the word that best completes each sentence.

1. The new luxury automobile was very (capacious, credence).
2. The judge gave little (coincidence, credence) to the witness.
3. Applicants for the job were asked to submit their (captivate, credentials).
4. The newspaper provided minimum coverage of the (capable, incident).
5. The promises made by the politician were seldom (credible, capable).

Check your answers with the Key on page 141.

F SUPPLEMENTARY WRITING EXERCISE

The roots that were taught in this lesson are:

cid-	cap-	cred-

Write sentences in which you use each of the roots in a word in the sentence.

1. ____
2. ____
3. ____

A WRITING THE WORDS

A. Write these words on the blank lines.
Then say each word.

		Write
cordial	1.	______________
discord	2.	______________
accord	3.	______________
corporeal	4.	______________
corpulent	5.	______________
corpuscle	6.	______________
progenitor	7.	______________
genuine	8.	______________
congenial	9.	______________
generate	10.	______________

B. Each word contains a word root or word stem.
Write the word root or the word stem for each word.

1. ______________
2. ______________
3. ______________
4. ______________
5. ______________
6. ______________
7. ______________
8. ______________
9. ______________
10. ______________

THESE ROOTS HAVE MEANINGS RELATED TO **LIFE**.

cor-dial \ ˈkȯr-jəl \ *adj* [ME, fr. ML *cordialis*, fr. L *cord-*, *cor* heart – more at HEART] **1** : *obs* : of or relating to the heart : VITAL **2** : tending to revive, cheer, or invigorate **3** : warmly and genially affable : HEARTFELT <she received a most ~ welcome> ***syn*** see GRACIOUS ***ant*** uncordial - **cor-dial-ly** \ ˈkȯrj-(ə)lē \ *adv* – **cor-dial-ness** \ ˈkȯr-jəl-nəs \ *n*

cor-po-re-al \ kȯr-ˈpōr-ē-əl, ˈpȯr- \ *adj* [L *corporeus* of the body, fr. *corpor-*, *corpus*] **1** : having, consisting of, or relating to a physical material body : as **a** : not spiritual **b** : not immaterial or intangible ; SUBSTANTIAL **2** *archaic* : CORPORAL ***syn*** see MATERIAL ***ant*** see incorporeal **2** : see BODILY – **cor-po-re-al-ly** \ -ē-ə-lē \ *adv* – **cor-po-re-al-ness** *n*

pro-gen-i-tor \ prō-ˈjen-ət-ər, prə- \ *n* [ME, fr. MF *progeniteur*, fr. L *progenitor*, fr. *progenitus*, pp. of *progignere* to beget, fr. *pro-* forth + *gignere* to beget – more at KIN] **1 a** : an ancestor in the direct line : FOREFATHER **b** : a biologically ancestral form **2** : PRECURSOR, ORIGINATOR < ~*s* of socialist ideas – *Times Lit. Supp.*>

B USING CONTEXT CLUES

Place an X in front of each correct answer. The word may be used correctly in one or both of the sentences.

1. The hostess extended a cordial greeting to her guests means
   ___a. the hostess was very friendly.
   ___b. the hostess was very rude.

2. There was discord between the two boys means
   ___a. there was a vast age difference between the two boys.
   ___b. the two boys had a difference of opinion about something.

3. The boy went to school of his own accord means
   ___a. he went without being asked.
   ___b. his parents forced him to go to school.

4. The corpulent teenager was often teased by her classmates
   ___a. because she was skinny.
   ___b. because she was fat.

5. A corpuscle is
   ___a. a very tiny blood cell.
   ___b. a very small star.

Check your answers with the Key on page 141.

C CHECKING THE MEANING

Read the words in the boxes. Choose the word that best completes the sentence under them. Write that word on the line. Then complete the next sentence by placing an X in front of the correct answer.

1. corpuscle progenitor

A family tree contains each ______________________ of the family.
This sentence means
___a. it contains all the ancestors in the direct family line.
___b. it contains only female ancestors.
___c. it contains only male ancestors.

2. genuine corpulent

The antique painting was found to be ______________________.
This sentence means
___a. the painting was fraudulent.
___b. the painting was a true antique.
___c. the painting was a cheap reproduction.

3. discord congenial

The two girls were ____________________ companions.
This sentence means
___a. they got along very well.
___b. they had little in common.
___c. they were often arguing.

4. corporeal cordial

Water, food, and shelter are all ______________________ needs.
This sentence means
___a. water, food, and shelter are all bodily needs that must be met.
___b. water, food, and shelter are not essential for survival.
___c. water, food, and shelter are needs that are difficult to meet.

5. generate accord

Steam is often used to ____________________ electrical power.
This sentence means
___a. steam is often used as an alternative to electricity.
___b. steam is a useless source of power.
___c. steam is often used to produce electricity

Check your answers with the Key on page 141.

SEQUENCE 9-14

D COMPLETING THE SENTENCES

Choose a word from the box that best completes each sentence. Write it on the line.

cordial	accord	corpuscle	congenial
discord	corpulent	corporeal	genuine

1. Overeating may cause a person to become ______________________.

2. The four-carat diamond was ______________________.

3. A host and hostess must extend a ________________ welcome to their guests.

4. The man and his co-worker had a very ____________________ relationship.

5. A red ____________________ carries oxygen and food throughout the body.

Check your answers with the Key on page 141.

E USING THE SKILL

Underline the word that best completes each sentence.

1. The two lawyers were in (corporate, accord) with one another.

2. Husbands and wives experience (congenial, discord) on occasion.

3. Clothing provides (corpuscle, corporeal) protection from the elements.

4. One (genuine, progenitor) of the family was a very famous historical figure.

5. Water pressure can be used to (generate, genuine) power.

Check your answers with the Key on page 141.

F SUPPLEMENTARY WRITING EXERCISE.

The roots that were taught in this lesson are:

cord-	corp-	gen-

Write sentences in which you use each of the roots in a word in the sentence.

1. ____

2. ____

3. ____

A WRITING THE WORDS

A. Write these words on the blank lines.
Then say each word.

Write

admonish	1.	____________
monitor	2.	____________
premonition	3.	____________
petition	4.	____________
competent	5.	____________
impetuous	6.	____________
complement	7.	____________
implement	8.	____________
supplement	9.	____________
deplete	10.	____________

B. Each word contains a word root or word stem. Write the word root or the word stem for each word.

1. ____________
2. ____________
3. ____________
4. ____________
5. ____________
6. ____________
7. ____________
8. ____________
9. ____________
10. ____________

THESE ROOTS HAVE MEANINGS RELATED TO AN **ACTION**.

de-plete \ di-ˈplēt \ *vt* **de-plet-ed; de-plet-ing** [L *depletus*, pp. of *deplēre*, fr. *de-* + *plēre* – more at FULL] 1 : to empty of a principal substance 2 : to lessen markedly in quantity, content, power, or value – **de-plet-able** \ -ˈplēt-ə-bəl \ *adj* – **de-ple-tion** \ -ˈplē-shən \ *n* – **de-ple-tive** \ -ˈplēt-iv \ *adj* ***syn*** DRAIN, EXHAUST, IMPOVERISH, BANKRUPT *shared meaning element* : to deprive of something essential to existence or potency

pe-ti-tion \ pə-ˈtish-ən \ *n* [ME, fr. MF, fr. L *petition-, petitio,* fr. *petitus*, pp. of *petere* to seek, request – more at FEATHER] **1** : an earnest request : ENTREATY **2 a** : a formal written request made to a superior **b** : a document embodying such a formal written request **3** : something asked or requested – **pe-ti-tion-ary** \ -ˈtish-ə- ner-ē \ *adj*

pre-mo-ni-tion \ prē-mə-ˈnish-ən, ˌprem-ə- \ *n* [MF, fr. LL *praemonition-, praemonitio,* fr. L *praemonitus*, pp. of *praemonēre* to warn in advance, fr. *pra* prē + *monere* to warn – more at MIND] **1** : previous notice or warning : FOREWARNING **2** : anticipation of an event without conscious reason : PRESENTIMENT

B USING CONTEXT CLUES

Place an X in front of each correct answer. The word may be used correctly in one or both of the sentences.

1. A parent will often admonish a child means
   ___a. a parent will often spank a child.
   ___b. a parent will often warn or advise his child.

2. The woman had a premonition means
   ___a. she was able to predict the future.
   ___b. she had a forewarning about things to come.

3. The teacher served as a monitor for her students means
   ___a. she helped her students by giving them advice.
   ___b. she served as a sort of baby-sitter.

4. The chef was very competent means
   ___a. he was very well qualified.
   ___b. he was very careless.

5. The student council candidate circulated a petition means
   ___a. he circulated a formal request to run for office.
   ___b. he paid students to vote for him.

Check your answers with the Key on page 141.

C CHECKING THE MEANING

Read the words in the boxes. Choose the word that best completes the sentence under them. Write that word on the line. Then complete the next sentence by placing an X in front of the correct answer.

1. | monitor | | impetuous |

He was an ______________________ person.
This sentence means
___a. he often acted hastily.
___b. he was on overly cautious person.
___c. he was very lazy.

2. | implement | | competent |

A soldier is always expected to ________________________ given orders.
This sentence means
___a. he is expected to forget orders once in a while.
___b. he is expected to receive a given order and carry it out.
___c. he is expected to improve the orders he is given.

3. | premonition | | deplete |

We must be careful not to ________________________ the school's paper supply.
This sentence means
___a. we must be sure there is always paper available.
___b. new paper must be ordered.
___c. no attention should be paid to the paper supply.

4. | complement | | monitor |

The bus had its full ____________________________ of passengers.
This sentence means
___a. more passengers could be added to the bus.
___b. the bus was empty.
___c. the bus was full.

5. | supplement | | deplete |

The teacher was able to _________________ classroom materials with library media.
This sentence means
___a. she felt library materials were better.
___b. she used library materials to improve and add to classroom materials.
___c. she replaced classroom materials with library materials.

Check your answers with the Key on page 141.

D COMPLETING THE SENTENCES

Choose a word from the box that best completes each sentence. Write it on the line.

admonish	monitor	petition	implement
deplete	competent	impetuous	premonition

1. We must be careful not to ________________________ our natural resources.
2. Students are expected to _____________________rules outside of the classroom.
3. Angry parents circulated a ____________________ to reinstate the fired teacher.
4. An _____________________ person often makes poor decisions.
5. The surgeon was a very ______________________ one.

Check your answers with the Key on page 141.

E USING THE SKILL

Underline the word that best completes each sentence.

1. A student was asked to (deplete, monitor) the class.
2. Mother said she had had a (competent, premonition) of the tragic accident.
3. It is necessary to (admonish, supplement) children when they are bad.
4. Vitamins are a good dietary (implement, supplement).
5. The grandfather clock was the perfect (complement, monitor) for the room.

Check your answers with the Key on page 141.

F SUPPLEMENTARY WRITING EXERCISE

The roots that were taught in this lesson are:

mon-	pet-	ple-

Write sentences in which you use each of the roots in a word in the sentence.

1. ____
2. ____
3. ____

A WRITING THE WORDS

Write these words on the blank lines.
Then say each word.

Write

complex	1.	______________
duplex	2.	______________
complexion	3.	______________
implicate	4.	______________
duplicate	5.	______________
complicate	6.	______________
replicate	7.	______________
implicit	8.	______________
explicit	9.	______________
complicity	10.	______________

B. Each word contains a word root or word stem. Write the word root or the word stem for each word.

1. ______________
2. ______________
3. ______________
4. ______________
5. ______________
6. ______________
7. ______________
8. ______________
9. ______________
10. ______________

THESE ROOTS HAVE MEANINGS RELATED TO **TWISTING** OR **TURNING**.

[1]**du-plex** \ ˈd(y)ü-, pleks \ *adj* [L, fr. *duo* two + *-plex* fold – more at TWO, SIMPLE] **1** : DOUBLE, TWOFOLD; *specif* : having two parts that operate at the same time or in the same way <a ~ lathe> **2** : allowing telecommunication in opposite directions simultaneously
[2]**duplex** *n* something duplex; *esp* : a two-family house
[3]**duplex** *vt* : to make duplex

com-pli-cate \ ˈkampləˌkāt \ *adj* [L *complicatus*, pp. of *complicare* to fold together, fr. *com-* + *plicare* to fold – more at PLY] **1** : COMPLEX, INTRICATE **2** : CONDUPLICATE *vb* -ED/-ING

im-plic-it \ im-ˈplis-ət \ *adj* [L *implicitus*, pp. of *implicare*] **1 a** : capable of being understood from something else though unexpressed : IMPLIED <an ~ assumption> **b** : involved in the nature or essence of something though not revealed, expressed, or developed : POTENTIAL <a sculptor may see different figures ~ in a block of stone – John Dewey> **2** : being without doubt or reserve : UNQUESTIONING, ABSOLUTE - **im-plic-it-ly** *adv* - **im-plic-it-ness** *n*

B USING CONTEXT CLUES

Place an X in front of each correct answer. The word may be used correctly in one or both of the sentences.

1. The family lives in a duplex means
   ___a. the family lives in a single-family dwelling.
   ___b. the family lives in a two-family dwelling.

2. The complexion of the problem changed quickly means
   ___a. the problem changed in one way.
   ___b. the problem changed in many ways.

3. The changing complexion may complicate the problem means
   ___a. the problem may become more difficult.
   ___b. the problem may become more involved.

4. A teacher must give explicit instructions means
   ___a. the teacher must give general instructions.
   ___b. the teacher must give exact instructions.

5. The scientist must replicate the experiment means
   ___a. the experiment must be completed.
   ___b. the experiment must be done over.

Check your answers with the Key on page 142.

C CHECKING THE MEANING

Read the words in the boxes. Choose the word that best completes the sentence under them. Write that word on the line. Then complete the next sentence by placing an X in front of the correct answer.

1. complex   complexion

The problem in biology became ____________________.
This sentence means
___a. the problem was easily solved.
___b. the problem was difficult to solve.
___c. the problem was made up of many parts.

2. duplicate   implicate

Do not ____________________ your friends in the crime.
This sentence means
___a. do not ask your friends about the crime.
___b. do not speak to your friends about the crime.
___c. do not involve your friends in the crime.

3. implicit   complicity

Your ____________________ in the crime makes you guilty.
This sentence means
___a. your participation in the crime makes you guilty.
___b. your lying about the crime makes you guilty.
___c. your telling about the crime makes you guilty.

4. complicate   replicate

You can, if necessary, ____________________ the experiment.
This sentence means
___a. you can gain results from the experiment.
___b. you can stop the experiment.
___c. you can repeat the experiment.

5. duplex   explicit

The doctor gave ____________________ instructions to the patient.
This sentence means
___a. the doctor examined the patient.
___b. the doctor diagnosed the patient.
___c. the doctor told the patient exactly what to do.

Check your answers with the Key on page 142.

D COMPLETING THE SENTENCES

Choose a word from the box that best completes each sentence. Write it on the line.

duplicate	complex	implicate	complicity
duplex	replicate	explicit	complexion

1. The machine will ______________________ the original manuscript.
2. A person's ____________________ changes as the seasons change.
3. The teacher's directions were ______________________.
4. A wise man does not ______________________anyone when an error is made.
5. Your _______________________ in the act implicates you.

Check your answers with the Key on page 142.

E USING THE SKILL

Underline the word that best completes each sentence.

1. The (complexion, complex) problem was difficult to solve.
2. I will (implicate, explicit) you for your part in the crime.
3. The student tried to (replicate, implicate) the manuscript.
4. We were given (implicit, explicit) directions to the store so we wouldn't get lost.
5. Always make a (duplex, duplicate) set of car keys.

Check your answers with the Key on page 142.

F SUPPLEMENTARY WRITING EXERCISE

The roots that were taught in this lesson are:

-plex	-plic	-plicit

Write sentences in which you use each of the roots in a word in the sentence.

1. ____
2. ____
3. ____

A WRITING THE WORDS

A. Write these words on the blank lines.
Then say each word.

Write

tangle	1.	______________
tangent	2.	______________
tangible	3.	______________
tact	4.	______________
tactile	5.	______________
contact	6.	______________
tenet	7.	______________
tenant	8.	______________
tendency	9.	______________
tenacious	10.	______________

B. Each word contains a word root or word stem.
Write the word root or the word stem for each word.

1. ______________
2. ______________
3. ______________
4. ______________
5. ______________
6. ______________
7. ______________
8. ______________
9. ______________
10. ______________

THESE ROOTS HAVE MEANINGS RELATED TO **TOUCH** OR TO **HOLD**.

tac-tile \ ˈtak-tᵊl, -ˌtīl \ *adj* [F or L; F, fr. L *tactilis,* fr. *tactus*, pp. of *tangere* to touch – more at TANGENT] **1** : perceptible by touch : TANGIBLE **2** : of or relating to the sense of touch – **tac-tile-ly** \ -tə-lē, -ˌtīl-lē \ *adv*

tan-gi-ble \ ˈtan-jə-bəl \ *adj* [LL *tangibles*, fr. L *tangere* to touch] **1 a** : capable of being perceived *esp*. by the sense of touch : PALPABLE **b** : substantially real : MATERIAL **2** : capable of being precisely realized by the mind **3** : capable of being appraised at an actual or approximate value <~assets> ***syn*** see PERCEPTIBLE ***ant*** intangible – **tan-gi-bil-i-ty** \ˌtan-jə-ˈbil-ət-ē \ *n* **tan-gi-ble-ness** \ ˈtan-jə-bəl-nəs \ *n* - **tan-gi-bly** \ -blē \ *adv*

te-net \ ten-ət *also* te-nət \ *n* [L, he holds, fr. *tenere* to hold] : a principle, belief, or doctrine generally held to be true; *esp.* : one held in common by members of an organization, group, movement, or profession ***syn*** see DOCTRINE

B USING CONTEXT CLUES

Place an X in front of each correct answer. The word may be used correctly in one or both of the sentences.

1. You will receive tangible rewards for your hard work means
   ___a. you will receive a reward that is changeable.
   ___b. you will receive a reward that is real.

2. I tried to contact you last night means
   ___a. I tried to reach you last night.
   ___b. I tried to acknowledge you last night.

3. The doctor has a tendency to be late means
   ___a. the doctor has a habit of being late.
   ___b. the doctor has established a pattern of being late.

4. The blind are sometimes tactile means
   ___a. the blind rely upon their sense of smell.
   ___b. the blind rely upon their sense of touch.

5. A basic tenet of the Constitution is freedom of speech means
   ___a. a basic principle is freedom of speech.
   ___b. a basic belief held by many in common.

Check your answers with the Key on page 142.

C CHECKING THE MEANING

Read the words in the boxes. Choose the word that best completes the sentence under them. Write that word on the line. Then complete the next sentence by placing an X in front of the correct answer.

1. tangible   tangent

The plan is ____________________ to our needs.
This sentence means
___a. the plan is irrelevant to our needs.
___b. the plan fulfills our needs.
___c. the plan is worthless for anyone's needs.

2. tact   tenant

Much ____________________ is needed to handle an irate person.
This sentence means
___a. one must be careful in handling an irate person.
___b. one must use common sense and diplomacy in handling an irate person.
___c. one must become involved with an irate person.

3. tangle   tact

A snare is a good means to ____________________ small game.
This sentence means
___a. a snare can hold small game.
___b. a snare can kill small game.
___c. a snare can obliterate small game.

4. tenacious   contact

An octopus is a very ____________________ creature.
This sentence means
___a. an octopus is a delicate creature.
___b. an octopus is an evil creature.
___c. an octopus holds fast to what it wants.

5. tangible   tenet

The belief in freedom of religion is a ____________________ of American life.
This sentence means
___a. freedom of religion is a basic principle of American life.
___b. freedom of religion is granted.
___c. freedom of religion is required by law.

Check your answers with the Key on page 142.

D COMPLETING THE SENTENCES

Choose a word from the box that best completes each sentence. Write it on the line.

tangible	tangent	contact	tendency
tenant	tactile	tenacious	tact

1. The money was a ______________________ reward for a job well done.
2. The homeowner was looking for a responsible __________________to rent her house.
3. The dog was ____________________ in holding on to its bone.
4. The _______________________to speak correctly comes with education and age.
5. Feeling the bark of a tree is a ______________________ impression.

Check your answers with the Key on page 142.

E USING THE SKILL

Underline the word that best completes each sentence.

1. The method of development is (tangent, tenet) to the method in the book.
2. Use a great deal of (tactile, tact) when speaking with the elderly.
3. The will to win requires a (tenacious, tendency) personality.
4. Small boys have a (tenet, tendency) to tease girls.
5. The (tenet, tenant) bought the house after ten years.

Check your answers with the Key on page 142.

F SUPPLEMENTARY WRITING EXERCISE

The roots that were taught in this lesson are:

tang-	tact-	ten-

Write sentences in which you use each of the roots in a word in the sentence.

1. ____
2. ____
3. ____

A WRITING THE WORDS

A. Write these words on the blank lines.
Then say each word.

	Write
description	1. ______________
prescription	2. ______________
inscription	3. ______________
transcription	4. ______________
preserve	5. ______________
reservation	6. ______________
reservoir	7. ______________
advisor	8. ______________
visual	9. ______________
television	10. ______________

B. Each word contains a word root or word stem.
Write the word root or the word stem for each word.

1. ______________
2. ______________
3. ______________
4. ______________
5. ______________
6. ______________
7. ______________
8. ______________
9. ______________
10. ______________

THESE ROOTS HAVE MEANINGS RELATED TO **ACTIONS**.

pre-scribe \ pri-ˈskrīb \ *vb* **pre-scribed; pre-scrib-ing** [ME *prescriben* L *praescribere* to write at the beginning, dictate, order, fr. *prae-* + *scribere* to write – more at SCRIBE] **1** : to claim a title to something by right of prescription **2** : to lay down a rule : DICTATE **3** : to write or give medical prescriptions **4** : to become by prescription invalid or unenforceable ~ *vt* **1 a** : to lay down as a guide, direction, or rule of action : ORDAIN **b** : to specify with authority **2** : to designate or order the use of as a remedy – **pre-scrib-er** *n*

pre-serve \ pri-ˈzərv \ *vb* **pre-served; pre-serv-ing** [ME, *preserven*, fr. MF *preserver*, fr. ML *praeservare*, fr. LL, to observe beforehand, fr. L *prae-* + *sevare* to keep, guard, observe – more at CONSERVE] *vt* **1** : to keep safe from injury, harm, or destruction : PROTECT **2 a** : to keep alive, intact, or free from decay **b** : MAINTAIN **3 a** : to keep or save from decomposition **b** : to can, pickle, or similarly prepare for future use **4** : to keep up and reserve for personal or special use ~ *vi* **1** : to make preserves **2** : to raise and protect game for purposes of sport **3** : to stand preserving (as by canning) ***syn*** see SAVE – **pre-serv-able** \ -ˈzər-və-bəl \ *adj* – **pres-er-va-tion** \ prez-ər-ˈvā-shən \ *n* – **pre-serv-er** \pri- ˈzər-vər \

vi-su-al \ˈvizh-(ə-)wəl, ˈvizh-əl \ *adj* [ME, fr. LL *visualis*, fr. L *visus* sight, fr. *visus*, pp. of *vidēre* to see] **1** : of, relating to, or used in vision < ~ organs> **2** : attained or maintained by sight < ~ impressions> **3** : OPTICAL <the ~ focus of a lens> **4** : VISIBLE **5** : producing mental images : VIVID **6** : done or executed by sight only < ~ navigation> **7** : of, relating to, or employing visual aids – **vi-su-al-ly** \ˈvizh-(ə-)wə-lē, ˈvizh-(ə-) lē \ *adv*

B USING CONTEXT CLUES

Place an X in front of each correct answer. The word may be used correctly in one or both of the sentences.

1. They had a <u>visual</u> image of the individual means
   ___a. they could not see the individual.
   ___b. they could see the individual.

2. The <u>television</u> receiver is a device that allows
   ___a. one to see pictures.
   ___b. one to see images from far away.

3. We had a dinner <u>reservation</u> means
   ___a. dinner was served promptly.
   ___b. a table was set aside for us.

4. The animals were kept on a wildlife <u>reservation</u> means
   ___a. the animals were kept on land set aside by the public.
   ___b. the animals were kept in pens.

5. The <u>inscription</u> on the bracelet was blurred means
   ___a. the words etched into the bracelet were blurred.
   ___b. the words painted on the bracelet could not be read.

Check your answers with the Key on page 142.

C CHECKING THE MEANING

Read the words in the boxes. Choose the word that best completes the sentence under them. Write that word on the line. Then complete the next sentence by placing an X in front of the correct answer.

1. | visual | | television |

The company made a ______________________ to advertise its product.
This sentence means
___a. the company carried out a campaign to advertise its product.
___b. the company made a deal to advertise its product.
___c. the company made an eye-catching picture to advertise its product.

2. | visual | | preserve |

We ____________________ freedom by defending it against foes.
This sentence means
___a. freedom is lost by defending it.
___b. freedom is saved by defending it.
___c. freedom is thought about by defending it.

3. | reservoir | | reservation |

The lake in the park is really a ______________________.
This sentence means
___a. the water will be used in the future.
___b. the lake stores water for swimming.
___c. the lake stores water for boating.

4. | inscription | | prescription |

The physician wrote a ______________________ for the medication.
This sentence means
___a. the physician wrote a diagnosis.
___b. the physician wrote the operating schedule.
___c. the physician wrote medication instructions.

5. | description | | transcription |

The secretary wrote a ______________________ of the shorthand into English.
This sentence means
___a. the secretary made a recording of the shorthand.
___b. the secretary made a visual of the shorthand.
___c. the secretary copied the shorthand into English.

Check your answers with the Key on page 142.

D COMPLETING THE SENTENCES

Choose a word from the box that best completes each sentence. Write it on the line.

television	description	reservoir	inscription
visual	preserve	reservation	transcription

1. The advertising man wrote a ________________ of the new product.
2. Mother will ________________ the peaches so we'll have them all winter.
3. The disc jockey played a ________________ of the new song.
4. A good ________________ takes the place of many words.
5. The ________________ was deeply etched into the stone.

Check your answers with the Key on page 142.

E USING THE SKILL

Underline the word that best completes each sentence.

1. The city must have a (reservation, reservoir) for future water needs.
2. Nora's (inscription, description) of the getaway car left out no details.
3. A (inscription, prescription) must be written before the medicine can be dispensed.
4. My uncle is an (advisor, inscription) to the President.
5. The (visual, television) of the plan made it easy to understand.

Check your answers with the Key on page 142.

F SUPPLEMENTARY WRITING EXERCISE

The roots that were taught in this lesson are:

scrip-	serv-	vis-

Write sentences in which you use each of the roots in a word in the sentence.

1. ________________________________
2. ________________________________
3. ________________________________

A WRITING THE WORDS

A. Write these words on the blank lines.
Then say each word.

		Write
convene	1.	____________________
convention	2.	____________________
convenience	3.	____________________
obverse	4.	____________________
inversion	5.	____________________
reversion	6.	____________________
conversion	7.	____________________
provoke	8.	____________________
revoke	9.	____________________
invoke	10.	____________________

B. Each word contains a word root or root stem.
Write the word root or the word stem for each word.

1. ____________________
2. ____________________
3. ____________________
4. ____________________
5. ____________________
6. ____________________
7. ____________________
8. ____________________
9. ____________________
10. ____________________

THESE ROOTS HAVE MEANINGS RELATED TO AN **ACTION**.

con-vene \ kən-ˈvēn \ *vb* **con-vened; con-ven-ing** [ME *convenen*, fr. MF *convenir* to come together] *vi* : to come together in a body ~ *vt* **1** : to summon before a tribunal **2** : to cause to assemble

ob-verse \ äb-ˈvərs, əb-, ˈäb-, \ *adj* [L *obversus*, fr. pp. of *obvertere* to turn toward, fr. *ob-* toward + *vertere* to turn – more at OB-. WORTH] **1** : facing the observer or opponent **2** : having the base narrower than the top <an ~ leaf> **3** : constituting a counterpart or complement - **ob-verse-ly** *adv*

pro-voke \ prə -ˈvōk \ vt **pro-voked; pro-vok-ing** [ME *provoken*, fr. MF *provoquer*, fr. L *provocare*, fr. *pro-* forth + *vocare* to call – more at PRO-, VOICE] **1 a** : *archaic* : AROUSE, STIR **b** : to incite to anger : INCENSE **2 a** : to call forth : EVOKE **b** : to stir up purposely : INDUCE **c** : to provide the needed stimulus for ***syn*** **1** : PROVOKE, EXCITE, STIMULATE, PIQUE, QUICKEN *shared meaning element* : to rouse one into doing or feeling or to produce by so rousing a person ***ant*** gratify **2** : see IRRITATE

B USING CONTEXT CLUES

Place an X in front of each correct answer. The word may be used correctly in one or both of the sentences.

1. The Congress will convene in January means
   ___a. Congress will complete its business in January.
   ___b. Congress will come together in January.

2. The conversion was made from coal to gas means
   ___a. a change was made from coal to gas.
   ___b. gas would now be used instead of coal.

3. A plaque can be fund on the obverse side of the building means
   ___a. the plaque is on the rear of the building.
   ___b. the plaque is on the main side of the building.

4. They did all they could to provoke an argument means
   ___a. they purposely tried to stop an argument.
   ___b. they purposely tried to start an argument.

5. They tried to invoke the teacher into helping means
   ___a. they tried to coerce the teacher into helping them.
   ___b. they asked the teacher for help and for support.

Check your answers with the Key on page 143.

C CHECKING THE MEANING

Read the words in the boxes. Choose the word that best completes the sentence under them. Write that word on the line. Then complete the next sentence by placing an X in front of the correct answer.

1. | convene | | convenience |

The elevator was a __________________ for the older people living in the building.
This sentence means
___a. the elevator made it more difficult for old people.
___b. the elevator made it less difficult for old people.
___c. the elevator was not appreciated.

2. | convention | | conversion |

A __________________ for mechanics was held in March.
This sentence means
___a. mechanics completed their business.
___b. mechanics worked on their jobs.
___c. mechanics came together in a meeting.

3. | reversion | | inversion |

The typist made an __________________ of the words on the page.
This sentence means
___a. the typist changed the meaning of the words on the page.
___b. the typist made a transcription of the words on the page.
___c. the typist changed the order of the words on the page.

4. | obverse | | invoke |

The __________________ of that statement is more correct.
This sentence means
___a. the basis of that statement is true.
___b. the opposite of that statement is true.
___c. the statement will never be believed.

5. | revoke | | provoke |

The judge will __________________ the man's driver's license.
This sentence means
___a. the judge will fine the driver.
___b. the judge will sentence the driver.
___c. the judge will take the man's driver's license away.

Check your answers with the Key on page 143.

D COMPLETING THE SENTENCES

Choose a word from the box that best completes each sentence. Write it on the line.

convene	reversion	provoke	revoke
inversion	invoke	convention	convenience

1. A group of students will ________________ to discuss the upcoming election.
2. The magic potion caused a complete ________________ of the aging process.
3. Every winter, the valley experiences a temperature ____________________.
4. The President may ______________ a diplomat's credentials at any time.
5. The student leader did much to _______________ the unrest of the student body.

Check your answers with the Key on page 143.

E USING THE SKILL

Underline the word that best completes each sentence.

1. A (convention, convene) was held to promote book sales.
2. The car's (reversion, conversion) proved to be popular with teenagers.
3. The (invoke, obverse) side of the coin is damaged.
4. The parent will (invoke, revoke) the stubborn child's privileges.
5. A (convenience, convene) store is located down the street.

Check your answers with the Key on page 143.

F SUPPLEMENTARY WRITING EXERCISE

The roots that were taught in this lesson are:

ven-	vers-	voke-

Write sentences in which you use each of the roots in a word in the sentence.

1. ____
2. ____
3. ____

A WRITING THE WORDS

A. Write these words on the blank lines. Then say each word.

Write

vivacious	1.	____________
vivid	2.	____________
convivial	3.	____________
revive	4.	____________
lucid	5.	____________
elucidate	6.	____________
translucent	7.	____________
luminous	8.	____________
luminary	9.	____________
illuminate	10.	____________

B. Each word contains a word root or word stem. Write the word root or the word stem for each word.

1. ____________
2. ____________
3. ____________
4. ____________
5. ____________
6. ____________
7. ____________
8. ____________
9. ____________
10. ____________

THESE ROOTS HAVE MEANINGS RELATED TO **LIGHT** AND **LIFE**.

con-viv-ial \ kən-ˈviv-yəl, -ˈviv-ē-əl \ *adj* [LL *convivialis*, fr. L *convivium* banquet, fr. *com-* + *vivere* to live – more at QUICK] : relating to, occupied with, or fond of feasting, drinking, and good company – **con-viv-i-al-i-ty** \ -viv-ē-ˈal-ət-ē \ *n* – **con-viv-ial-ly** \ -ˈviv-yə-lē, -ˈviv-ē-ə-lē \ *adv*

[1]il-lu-mi-nate \ ˈil- ü-mə-nət \ *adj* **1** *archaic* : brightened with light **2** *archaic* : intellectually or spiritually enlightened
[2]il-lu-mi-nate \ -nāt \ *vt* **-nat-ed; -nat-ing** [L *illuminatus*, pp. of *illuminare*, fr. *in-* + *luminare* to light up, fr. *lumin-*, *lumen* light – more at LUMINARY] **1 a** : (1) : to supply or brighten with light (2) : to make luminous or shining **b** : to enlighten spiritually or intellectually **c** *archaic* : to set alight **d** : to subject to radiation

trans-lu-cent \ -ᵊnt \ *adj* [L *translucent-*, *translucens*, prp. of *translucēre* to shine through, fr. *trans-* + *lucere* to shine – more at LIGHT] **1** : permitting the passage of light: **a** : CLEAR, TRANSPARENT <the water was ~, and I could readily watch from the side of the canoe what was going on – V.G. Heiser> **b** : transmitting and diffusing light so that objects beyond cannot be seen clearly <which looks like honey, ~ and sunny, from clover-tops – Elinor Wylie> **2** : free from disguise or falseness <his ~ patriotism – *Newsweek*> <gave one of her ~ performances of a dreaming, wounded...young girl – Stark Young> – **trans-lu-cent-ly** *adv*

B USING CONTEXT CLUES

Place an X in front of each correct answer. The word may be used correctly in one or both of the sentences.

1. It was a convivial occasion means
 ___a. it was suitable for having a feast or banquet.
 ___b. it was an occasion for mourning.

2. An attempt was made to revive the half-drowned child means
 ___a. an attempt was made to bring the child back to consciousness.
 ___b. an attempt was made to feed the child.

3. She was a vivacious young lady means
 ___a. she was a timid girl.
 ___b. she was a lively girl.

4. The colors in the painting were vivid means
 ___a. the colors were soft and delicate.
 ___b. the colors were brilliant.

5. The assembly instructions were lucid means
 ___a. they were easy to understand.
 ___b. they were very confusing.

Check your answers with the Key on page 143.

C CHECKING THE MEANING

Read the words in the boxes. Choose the word that best completes the sentence under them. Write that word on the line. Then complete the next sentence by placing an X in front of the correct answer.

1. revive elucidate

Scientific experiments help to ________________________ scientific theories.
This sentence means
___a. experiments do not prove theories.
___b. experiments help clarify theories.
___c. experiments have no relationship to theories.

2. luminary lucid

Both the sun and the moon are ______________________ bodies.
This sentence means
___a. they give off light.
___b. they give off heat.
___c. they can only be seen with a telescope.

3. illuminate elucidate

Candles were used to ___________________________ the church.
This sentence means
___a. candles were used to heat the church.
___b. candles were used in ceremonies.
___c. candles were used to light the church.

4. lucid luminous

A light bulb is an object that illuminates but is not ______________________.
This sentence means
___a. the light bulb does not work.
___b. it does not shine by itself.
___c. it shines by itself.

5. luminous translucent

Frosted windows in a home are ____________________.
This sentence means
___a. frosted windows will allow light to pass through.
___b. frosted windows will not allow light to pass through.
___c. frosted windows are transparent.

Check your answers with the Key on page 143.

D COMPLETING THE SENTENCES

Choose a word from the box that best completes each sentence. Write it on the line.

lucid	vivacious	convivial	translucent
vivid	revive	elucidate	luminary

1. The young puppy had a ______________________ spirit.
2. The results of the scientific experiment were very _________________.
3. Thanksgiving Day is a very _____________________ occasion.
4. The nurse tried to ___________________ the girl who had fainted.
5. The interior designer chose ______________________ colors for the room.

Check your answers with the Key on page 143.

E USING THE SKILL

Underline the word that best completes each sentence.

1. The door on the shower stall was made of (lucid, translucent) material.
2. High-power floodlights were used to (illuminate, lucid) the airport runway.
3. The moon is a (vivid, luminous) heavenly body.
4. The doctor was asked to (revive, elucidate) on the new surgical procedure.
5. The North Star is the only stationary (convivial, luminous) star.

Check your answers with the Key on page 143.

F SUPPLEMENTARY WRITING EXERCISE

The roots that were taught in this lesson are:

viv-	luc-	lumin-

Write sentences in which you use each of the roots in a word in the sentence.

1. ____
2. ____
3. ____

A WRITING THE WORDS

A. Write these words on the blank lines. Then say each word.

Write

betrayal	1.	______________
denial	2.	______________
refusal	3.	______________
abduction	4.	______________
abdication	5.	______________
calculation	6.	______________
diversity	7.	______________
disparity	8.	______________
eligibility	9.	______________
dissimilarity	10.	______________

B. Each word ends with a suffix. Write the suffix for each word.

1. ______________
2. ______________
3. ______________
4. ______________
5. ______________
6. ______________
7. ______________
8. ______________
9. ______________
10. ______________

THESE SUFFIXES HAVE MEANINGS RELATED TO **QUALITY** OR **CONDITION**.

^{1}**-al** \ əl, ^{ə}l \ *adj suffix* [ME, fr. OF & L; OF, fr. L *-alis*] : of, relating to, or characterized by <direction*al*> <fiction*al*>
^{2}**-al** *n suffix* [ME *-aille*, fr. OF, fr. L *-alia*, neut. pl. of *-alis*] : action : process <rehears*al*>
^{3}**-al** \ ˌal, ˌȯl, əl, ^{ə}l \ *n suffix* [F, fr. *alcool* alcohol, fr. ML *alcohol*] **1** : aldehyde <butan*al*> **2** : acetal <butyr*al*>

-ion *n suffix* [ME *-ioun, -ion*, fr. OF *-ion*, fr. L *-ion-, -io*] **1 a** : act or process <validat*ion*> **b** : result of an act or process <regulat*ion*> **2** : state or condition <hydrat*ion*>

-ty *n suffix* [ME *-te*, fr. OF *-té*, fr. L *-tat-, -tas* – more at ITY] : quality : condition : degree <a prior*ity*>

B USING CONTEXT CLUES

Place an X in front of each correct answer. The word may be used correctly in one or both of the sentences.

1. The man was disliked due to his <u>betrayal</u> of his friend means
   ___a. he was disloyal to his friend.
   ___b. he fought with his friend often.

2. The child's constant <u>denial</u> of the theft angered his mother means
   ___a. the child blamed the theft on someone else.
   ___b. the child would not admit to the crime.

3. The judge would not accept the man's <u>refusal</u> to testify means
   ___a. the man was not expected to testify.
   ___b. the man said he wouldn't testify.

4. The king's <u>abdication</u> created political turmoil means
   ___a. the king's decision to resign created turmoil.
   ___b. the king's decision to regain the throne created turmoil.

5. The <u>abduction</u> of the baby infuriated the neighborhood means
   ___a. the baby was kidnapped.
   ___b. the baby was very ill.

Check your answers with the Key on page 143.

C CHECKING THE MEANING

Read the words in the boxes. Choose the word that best completes the sentence under them. Write that word on the line. Then complete the next sentence by placing an X in front of the correct answer.

1. | calculation | | betrayal |

The accountant's ____________________ of the taxes was correct.
This sentence means
___a. the accountant seldom made mistakes.
___b. the accountant figured out the taxes correctly.
___c. the accountant never made mistakes.

2. | denial | | disparity |

There was a great deal of _________________ between the witnesses' stories.
This sentence means
___a. the stories were all different.
___b. the stories were similar.
___c. the witnesses did not tell the truth.

3. | eligibility | | abdication |

The man's __________________ for admission to the fraternity was questionable.
This sentence means
___a. the man was readily admitted to the fraternity.
___b. the man was not allowed to join the fraternity.
___c. the man's qualifications for admission were questionable.

4. | abduction | | diversity |

There was a _________________ of interests within the family.
This sentence means
___a. the family had a variety of interests.
___b. the family had no hobbies.
___c. everyone in the family shared the same interests.

5. | dissimilarity | | refusal |

Job opportunities for males and females must show no ____________________.
This sentence means
___a. opportunities must be the same for males and females.
___b. opportunities must be different for males and females.
___c. opportunities must improve for males and females.

Check your answers with the Key on page 143.

D COMPLETING THE SENTENCES

Choose a word from the box that best completes each sentence. Write it on the line.

betrayal	refusal	abduction	dissimilarity
denial	abdication	calculation	disparity

1. The king's ____________________ of his throne shocked the country.
2. The banker's ____________________ of the interest earned was too high.
3. The ____________________ of children in this country seems to be on the rise.
4. The boy's ____________________ to show up for practice made his coach angry.
5. The man was hanged after his ____________________ of the king.

Check your answers with the Key on page 143.

E USING THE SKILL

Underline the word that best completes each sentence.

1. The (denial, disparity) of abilities within the classroom created problems.
2. The professor's (denial, diversity) of interests made him popular.
3. The (denial, dissimilarity) of textures in the carpet made it beautiful.
4. The employer's (abduction, denial) of employee demands caused the strike.
5. Grades were the basis of (diversity, eligibility) for the scholarship.

Check your answers with the Key on page 143.

F SUPPLEMENTARY WRITING EXERCISE

The suffixes that were taught in this lesson are:

-al	-ion	-ty

Write sentences in which you use each of the suffixes in a word in the sentence.

1. ____
2. ____
3. ____

A WRITING THE WORDS

A. Write these words on the blank lines. Then say each word.

Write

exposure	1.	____________
fissure	2.	____________
immure	3.	____________
aviary	4.	____________
beneficiary	5.	____________
reactionary	6.	____________
observatory	7.	____________
conservatory	8.	____________
depository	9.	____________
repertory	10.	____________

B. Each word ends with a suffix. Write the suffix for each word.

1. ____________
2. ____________
3. ____________
4. ____________
5. ____________
6. ____________
7. ____________
8. ____________
9. ____________
10. ____________

THESE SUFFIXES HAVE MEANINGS RELATED TO **PROCESS**, **FUNCTION**, OR **PLACE**.

[1]**-ary** \ *US usu* ˌer-ē *when an unstressed syllable precedes,* ə-rē *or* rē *when a stressed syllable precedes; Brit usu* ə-rē *or* rē *in all cases n suffix* [ME *-arie*, fr. OF & L; OF *-aire, -arie*, fr. *-arius, -aria, -arium*, fr. *-arius*, adj. suffix] **1** : thing belonging to or connected with; *esp* : place of <ov*ary*> **2** : person belonging to, connected with, or engaged in <function*ary*>
[2]**-ary** *adj suffix* [ME *-arie*, fr. MF & L; MF *-aire*, fr. L *-arius*] : of, relating to, or connected with <budget*ary*>

[1]**-ory** \ ˌōr-ē, ˌȯr-ē, (ə-)rē \ *n suffix* [ME *-orie*, fr. L *-orium*, fr. neut. of *-orius*, adj suffix] **1** : place of or for <observat*ory*> **2** : something that serves for <cremat*ory*>
[2]**-ory** *adj suffix* [ME *-orie*, fr. MF & L; MF, fr. L *-orius*] **1** : of, relating to, or characterized by <gustat*ory*> **2** : serving for, producing, or maintaining <justificat*ory*>

-ure *n suffix* [ME, fr. OF, fr. L *-ura*] **1** : act : process <expos*ure*> **2** : office : function; *also* : body performing (such) a function <legislat*ure*>

B USING CONTEXT CLUES

Place an X in front of each correct answer. The word may be used correctly in one or both of the sentences.

1. Exposure of metal to moisture can cause rust means
   ___a. protecting metal from moisture causes rust.
   ___b. water coming in contact with metal may cause rust.

2. The fissure in the sidewalk made the man trip means
   ___a. a bump in the sidewalk made the man trip.
   ___b. a crack in the sidewalk made the man trip.

3. The judge planned to immure the man for his crimes means
   ___a. the judge planned to imprison the man.
   ___b. the judge dismissed the charges against the man.

4. The politician made a reactionary statement means
   ___a. he made a statement that favored a return to previous politics.
   ___b. he refrained from a political comment.

5. The zoo planned to construct a new aviary means
   ___a. the zoo would add a new reptile exhibit.
   ___b. the zoo would add a new bird exhibit.

Check your answers with the Key on page 144.

C CHECKING THE MEANING

Read the words in the boxes. Choose the word that best completes the sentence under them. Write that word on the line. Then complete the next sentence by placing an X in front of the correct answer.

1. depository | aviary

The book ____________________ contained thousands of books.
This sentence means
___a. the books were in a public library.
___b. the books were stored in a place for safekeeping.
___c. the books were stored before they were destroyed.

2. repertory | reactionary

The comedian's ______________________ of jokes seemed endless.
This sentence means
___a. he had a large collection of jokes.
___b. he knew very few jokes.
___c. he was an excellent entertainer.

3. observatory | immure

The man spent many hours in the ______________________ using the telescope.
This sentence means
___a. he spent many hours looking at the stars.
___b. he spent many hours practicing the piano.
___c. he spent many hours on genetic research.

4. conservatory | fissure

The student will enter a __________________ when he graduates from college.
This sentence means
___a. he plans to study music.
___b. he plans to study astronomy.
___c. he plans to study medicine.

5. exposure | beneficiary

A child is a __________________ of his parents' values and goals.
This sentence means
___a. parents often neglect their children.
___b. parents seldom help their children.
___c. children receive benefits from their parents.

Check your answers with the Key on page 144.

D COMPLETING THE SENTENCES

Choose a word from the box that best completes each sentence. Write it on the line.

aviary	immure	exposure	repertory
fissure	reactionary	beneficiary	observatory

1. To ______________________ someone without a fair trial is against the law.
2. The ______________________ was filled with exotic plants.
3. The ______________________ held hundreds of birds.
4. A great deal of money will go to the ______________________ of the man's estate.
5. A ______________________ was responsible for the weakened wall.

Check your answers with the Key on page 144.

E USING THE SKILL

Underline the word that best completes each sentence.

1. The lost hiker died of (fissure, exposure).
2. Steam escaped from the (immure, fissure) in the rock.
3. A (reactionary, aviary) often creates political conflicts.
4. The chef had a large (conservatory, repertory) of exotic recipes.
5. The gold (depository, beneficiary) was kept under strict security.

Check your answers with the Key on page 144.

F SUPPLEMENTARY WRITING EXERCISE

The suffixes that were taught in this lesson are:

-ure	-ary	-ory

Write sentences in which you use each of the suffixes in a word in the sentence.

1. ____
2. ____
3. ____

A WRITING THE WORDS

A. Write these words on the blank lines. Then say each word.

Write

abnormality	1.	____________
geniality	2.	____________
familiarity	3.	____________
infinity	4.	____________
aggressiveness	5.	____________
contrariness	6.	____________
tawdriness	7.	____________
impervious	8.	____________
melodious	9.	____________
malodorous	10.	____________

B. Each word ends with a suffix. Write the suffix for each word.

1. ____________
2. ____________
3. ____________
4. ____________
5. ____________
6. ____________
7. ____________
8. ____________
9. ____________
10. ____________

THESE SUFFIXES HAVE MEANINGS RELATED TO **STATE**, **QUALITY**, OR **CONDITION**.

SEQUENCE 9-23

-ity \ ət-ē \ *n suffix* [ME *-ite*, fr. OF or L; OF *-ité*, fr. L *-itat-*, *-itas*, fr. -i- (stem vowel of adjs.) + *-tat-*, *-tas* -ity; akin to Gk *-tēt-*, *-tēs* -ity] : quality : state : degree <alkalin*ity*> <theatrical*ity*>

-ness \ nəs \ *n suffix* [ME *-nes*, fr. OE; akin to OHG *-nissa* -ness] : state : condition: quality : degree <good*ness*>

-ous \ əs \ *adj suffix* [ME, partly fr. OF *-ous*, *-eus*, *-eux* fr. L *-osus*; partly fr. L *-us*, nom. sing. masc. ending of many adjectives] **1** : full of : abounding in : having : possessing the qualities of <clamor*ous*> <poison*ous*> **2** : having a valence lower than in compounds or ions named with an adjective ending in *-ic* <mercur*ous*>

B USING CONTEXT CLUES

Place an X in front of each correct answer. The word may be used correctly in one or both of the sentences.

1. The boy's tardiness was an <u>abnormality</u> for him means
   ___a. he was not usually tardy.
   ___b. he was always tardy.

2. The man's <u>familiarity</u> with the case released him from jury duty means
   ___a. he knew something about the case.
   ___b. he knew nothing about the case.

3. The <u>geniality</u> of the hostess helped to make the party a success means
   ___a. the hostess spent a great deal of money on the party.
   ___b. the hostess was warm and friendly.

4. The concept of <u>infinity</u> is hard to understand means
   ___a. something with established limits is hard to understand.
   ___b. something with no limits or bounds is hard to understand.

5. A <u>malodorous</u> smell drifted from the laboratory means
   ___a. an unpleasant odor drifted from the laboratory.
   ___b. a pleasant odor drifted from the laboratory.

Check your answers with the Key on page 144.

C CHECKING THE MEANING

Read the words in the boxes. Choose the word that best completes the sentence under them. Write that word on the line. Then complete the next sentence by placing an X in front of the correct answer.

1. | melodious | | malodorous |

The music played by the symphony was very ____________________.
This sentence means
___a. they symphony needed more practice.
___b. the music was not pleasing to the ear.
___c. the music was pleasant to listen to.

2. | familiarity | | aggressiveness |

Hockey players are known for their ______________________ while playing.
This sentence means
___a. they are known for rugged, energetic movements.
___b. they are known for restraint and control.
___c. they are known for graceful movements.

3. | contrariness | | geniality |

The _____________________ of people's views often starts an argument.
This sentence means
___a. all people share the same views.
___b. people enjoy arguing.
___c. people's opposing views often start an argument.

4. | tawdriness | | infinity |

The __________________ of the girl's dress made her the victim of much teasing.
This sentence means
___a. the girl dressed in an elegant fashion.
___b. the girl was very fashionable in her dress.
___c. the girl dressed in a gaudy way.

5. | impervious | | abnormality |

The raincoat was ______________________ to the rain.
This sentence means
___a. the raincoat absorbed the rain.
___b. the rain could not pass through the raincoat.
___c. rain was able to pass through the coat.

Check your answers with the Key on page 144.

D COMPLETING THE SENTENCES

Choose a word from the box that best completes each sentence. Write it on the line.

geniality	malodorous	impervious	abnormality
infinity	melodious	familiarity	contrariness

1. His ______________________ with the law helped him in his political ambitions.
2. The child was ______________________ to the constant teasing of his peers.
3. The girl's ______________________ made her very popular.
4. The math student was asked to write the symbol for ______________________.
5. The ______________________ in the boy's hearing had also impaired his speech.

Check your answers with the Key on page 144.

E USING THE SKILL

Underline the word that best completes each sentence.

1. A (malodorous, melodious) sound filled the air.
2. Her (contrariness, geniality) of opinion made her very unpopular.
3. The (contrariness, aggressiveness) of the enemy helped them win the war.
4. The (geniality, tawdriness) of the hotel attracted few customers.
5. Sauerkraut is known to be (melodious, malodorous).

Check your answers with the Key on page 144.

F SUPPLEMENTARY WRITING EXERCISE

The suffixes that were taught in this lesson are:

-ity	-ness	-ous

Write sentences in which you use each of the suffixes in a word in the sentence.

1. ____
2. ____
3. ____

A WRITING THE WORDS

A. Write these words on the blank lines. Then say each word.

Write

natural	1.	______________
marginal	2.	______________
nocturnal	3.	______________
communal	4.	______________
senile	5.	______________
reconcile	6.	______________
projectile	7.	______________
asteroid	8.	______________
spheroid	9.	______________
paranoid	10.	______________

B. Each word ends with a suffix. Write the suffix for each word.

1. ______________
2. ______________
3. ______________
4. ______________
5. ______________
6. ______________
7. ______________
8. ______________
9. ______________
10. ______________

THESE SUFFIXES HAVE MEANINGS THAT SHOW **RELATIONSHIP**.

[1]-al \ əl, ᵊl \ *adj suffix* [ME, fr. OF & L; OF, fr. L *-alis*] : of, relating to, or characterized by <direction*al*> <fiction*al*>
[2]-al *n suffix* [ME *-aille*, fr. OF, fr. L *-alia*, neut. pl. of *-alis*] : action : process <rehears*al*>
[3]-al \ ˌal, ˌȯl, ᵊl \ *n suffix* [F, fr. *alcool* alcohol, fr. ML *alcohol*] **1** : aldehyde <butan*al*> **2** : acetal <butyr*al*>

[1]-ile \ əl, ᵊl, ˌil, (ˌ)il \ *adj suffix* [ME, fr. MF, fr. L *-ilis*] : of, relating to, or capable of <contract*ile*>

[2]-ile *n suffix* [prob. fr. *-ile* (as in *quartile*, n.)] : segment of a (specified) size in a frequency distribution <dec*ile*>

-oid \ ˌȯid \ *n suffix* : something resembling a (specified) object or having a (specified) quality <glob*oid*>

B USING CONTEXT CLUES

Place an X in front of each correct answer. The word may be used correctly in one or both of the sentences.

1. Bats are nocturnal means
 ___a. bats are active during the day.
 ___b. bats are active during the night.

2. The farm is a communal operation means
 ___a. it is privately owned by a single individual.
 ___b. it is owned and operated jointly by a group of people.

3. Land marginal to the ocean is very expensive means
 ___a. land contained on an island is very expensive.
 ___b. land bordering an ocean is very expensive.

4. Crude oil is a valuable natural resource means
 ___a. crude oil is not man-made.
 ___b. crude oil is man-made.

5. The man has a senile condition means
 ___a. the man's condition is caused by old age.
 ___b. the man's condition is caused by a bad heart.

Check your answers with the Key on page 144.

C CHECKING THE MEANING

Read the words in the boxes. Choose the word that best completes the sentence under them. Write that word on the line. Then complete the next sentence by placing an X in front of the correct answer.

1. | projectile | | nocturnal |

The ______________________________ from the gun hit the target.
This sentence means
___a. an object shot from the gun hit the target.
___b. the gun hit the target.
___c. only an expert marksman should fire a gun.

2. | communal | | reconcile |

The separated couple attempted to ______________________ their differences.
This sentence means
___a. the couple made no attempt to settle their differences.
___b. the couple found their situation humorous.
___c. the couple tried to settle their differences.

3. | asteroid | | marginal |

The astronomer attempted to study the strange __________________ through the lens.
This sentence means
___a. he attempted to study an alien spaceship.
___b. he attempted to study a very small planet.
___c. he attempted to study the moon.

4. | paranoid | | natural |

The man was hospitalized due to his _________________________ character.
This sentence means
___a. the man suffered from a heart attack.
___b. the man suffered from a type of mental illness.
___c. the man was seldom in good health.

5. | spheroid | | projectile |

The ___________________ looked like an alien spaceship.
This sentence means
___a. the object was cigar-shaped.
___b. the object was saucer-shaped.
___c. the object was ball-shaped.

Check your answers with the Key on page 144.

D COMPLETING THE SENTENCES

Choose a word from the box that best completes each sentence. Write it on the line.

senile	marginal	nocturnal	reconcile
natural	asteroid	communal	projectile

1. Preparation for the annual rodeo is a ____________________ effort.
2. The family wanted a cabin built on land ____________________ to the lake.
3. As the man grew older, he became more ______________________.
4. The model had true ____________________ beauty.
5. The moon and stars are ______________________ sights.

Check your answers with the Key on page 144.

E USING THE SKILL

Underline the word that best completes each sentence.

1. The (senile, projectile) from the toy rocket hit the boy in the eye.
2. The (asteroid, communal) changed its orbit frequently.
3. A globe is a kind of (spheroid, asteroid).
4. A (asteroid, paranoid) individual often experiences delusions.
5. The prisoner hoped that, one day, he could (nocturnal, reconcile) with society.

Check your answers with the Key on page 144.

F SUPPLEMENTARY WRITING EXERCISE

The suffixes that were taught in this lesson are:

-al	-ile	-oid

Write sentences in which you use each of the suffixes in a word in the sentence.

1. ____
2. ____
3. ____

A WRITING THE WORDS

A. Write these words on the blank lines. Then say each word.

Write

restrictive	1.	______________
objective	2.	______________
subjective	3.	______________
signify	4.	______________
rectify	5.	______________
nullify	6.	______________
fraternize	7.	______________
monopolize	8.	______________
neutralize	9.	______________
nationalize	10.	______________

B. Each word ends with a suffix. Write the suffix for each word.

1. ______________
2. ______________
3. ______________
4. ______________
5. ______________
6. ______________
7. ______________
8. ______________
9. ______________
10. ______________

THESE SUFFIXES HAVE MEANINGS THAT RELATE TO AN **ACTION**, OR **RESULT OF AN ACTION**.

-fy \ ˌfī \ *vb suffix* [ME *-fien*, fr. L *-fiacre*, fr. *-ficus* -fic] **1** : make : form into <dandi*fy*> **2** : invest with the attributes of : make similar to <citi*fy*>

-ive \ iv \ *adj suffix* [ME *-if, -ive*, fr. MF & L; MF *-if*, fr. L *-ivus*] : that performs or tends toward an (indicated) action <abus*ive*>

-ize \ ˌīz \ *vb suffix* [ME *-isen*, fr. OF *-iser*, fr. LL *-izare*, fr. Gk *-izein*] **1 a** (1) : cause to be or conform to or resemble <system*ize*> <American*ize*> : cause to be formed into <union*ize*> (2) : subject to a (specified) action <plagiar*ize*> (3) : impregnant or treat or combine with <albumin*ize*> **b** : treat like <idol*ize*> **c** : treat according to the method of <bowdler*ize*> **2 a** : become : become like <crystal*ize*> **b** : be productive in or of <hypothes*ize*> : engage in a (specified) activity <philosoph*ize*> **c** : adopt or spread the manner of activity or the teaching of <Calvin*ize*>

B USING CONTEXT CLUES

Place an X in front of each correct answer. The word may be used correctly in one or both of the sentences.

1. The law was a restrictive one means
   ___a. the law prohibited something altogether.
   ___b. the law set certain limits and conditions.

2. The objective of the lesson is to learn to classify objects means
   ___a. the end result is to learn to classify objects.
   ___b. classifying objects is fascinating.

3. The man's opinion was subjective means
   ___a. the opinion reflected the man's thoughts and feelings.
   ___b. the opinion reflected the thoughts and feelings of someone else.

4. A bell will ring to signify the end of the meeting means
   ___a. the bell is the signal to adjourn the meeting.
   ___b. a bell is never used to end a meeting.

5. The banker wished to rectify his mistake means
   ___a. he would not admit to his mistake.
   ___b. he wished to correct his mistake.

Check your answers with the Key on page 145.

C CHECKING THE MEANING

Read the words in the boxes. Choose the word that best completes the sentence under them. Write that word on the line. Then complete the next sentence by placing an X in front of the correct answer.

1. fraternize | restrictive

The hired help was not allowed to ______________________ with the party guests.
This sentence means
___a. they were not allowed to socialize with the guests.
___b. they were allowed to socialize with the guests.
___c. they were allowed to eat with the guests.

2. monopolize | restrictive

A certain Arab nation planned to ______________________ the oil industry.
This sentence means
___a. the Arab nation planned to share its control of the oil industry.
___b. the Arab nation planned to release control of the oil.
___c. the Arab nation planned to gain control of the oil industry.

3. neutralize | rectify

A basic solution is used to ____________________ an acid solution.
This sentence means
___a. a base has no effect on an acid.
___b. a basic solution strengthens an acidic solution.
___c. a base will counteract the effects of an acid by diluting it.

4. signify | nullify

I wish to ____________________ my contract with the architect.
This sentence means
___a. I want to honor my contract.
___b. I want to cancel my contract.
___c. I want to renegotiate my contract.

5. nationalize | neutralize

The country plans to ____________________ its railroad system.
This sentence means
___a. the country plans to expand its railroad system.
___b. the country wants to own and control the railroad system.
___c. the country plans to close down the railroads.

Check your answers with the Key on page 145.

D COMPLETING THE SENTENCES

Choose a word from the box that best completes each sentence. Write it on the line.

signify	objective	monopolize	nationalize
nullify	fraternize	neutralize	restrictive

1. The General's ________________________ was to win the war.
2. Members could not ___________________ with members of another fraternity.
3. An attempt was made to _____________________ the company's contract.
4. The government planned to _______________________ the agricultural industry.
5. An antitoxin was used to _____________________ the rattlesnake venom.

Check your answers with the Key on page 145.

E USING THE SKILL

Underline the word that best completes each sentence.

1. The dam was built as a (subjective, restrictive) measure against flooding.
2. In marriage, a ring is used to (signify, nullify) a bond of love.
3. The company wished to (signify, rectify) the error posted to your account.
4. The couple asked the court to (signify, nullify) their marriage.
5. A person's belief in God is entirely (restrictive, subjective).

Check your answers with the Key on page 145.

F SUPPLEMENTARY WRITING EXERCISE

The suffixes that were taught in this lesson are:

-ive	-fy	-ize

Write sentences in which you use each of the suffixes in a word in the sentence.

1. ____
2. ____
3. ____

A WRITING THE WORDS

A. Write these words on the blank lines.
Then say each word.

Write

negotiate	1.	______________
articulate	2.	______________
obviate	3.	______________
amiable	4.	______________
remediable	5.	______________
accessible	6.	______________
credible	7.	______________
visage	8.	______________
forage	9.	______________
patronage	10.	______________

B. Each word ends with a suffix. Write the suffix for each word.

1. ______________
2. ______________
3. ______________
4. ______________
5. ______________
6. ______________
7. ______________
8. ______________
9. ______________
10. ______________

THESE SUFFIXES HAVE MEANINGS RELATED TO **CAUSE** AND **EFFECT**.

-able *also* **-ible** \ ə-b əl \ *adj suffix* [ME, fr. OF, fr. L *-abilis, -ibilis*, fr. *-a-, -i-*, verb stem vowels + *bilis* capable or worthy of] **1** : capable of, fit for, or worthy of (being so acted upon or toward) – chiefly in adjectives derived from verbs <break*able*> <collect*ible*> **2** : tending, given, or liable to <knowledge*able*> <perish*able*>

-age \ ij \ *n suffix* [ME, fr. OF, fr. L *-aticum*] **1** : aggregate : collection <track*age*> **2 a** : action : process <haul*age*> **b** : cumulative result of <break*age*> **c** : rate of <dos*age*> **3** : house or place of <orphan*age*> **4** : state : rank <peon*age*> **5** : fee : charge <post*age*>

¹-ate \ ət, ˌāt \ *n suffix* [ME *-at*, fr. OF, fr. L *-atus, -atum*, masc. & neut. of *-atus*, pp. ending] **1** : one acted upon (in a specified way) <distill*ate*> **2** [NL *-atum*, fr. L] : chemical compound or complex anion derived from a (specified) compound or element <phenol*ate*> <ferr*ate*>; *esp* : salt or ester of an acid with a name ending in *-ic* and not beginning with *hydro-* <bor*ate*>

²-ate *n suffix* [ME *-at*, fr. OF, fr. L *-atus*, pp. ending] : office : function : rank : group of persons holding a (specified) office or rank or having a (specified) function <vicar*ate*>

³-ate *adj suffix* [ME *-at*, fr. L *-atus*, fr. pp. ending of 1st conj. verbs, fr. *-a-*, stem vowel of 1st conj. + *-tus*, pp. suffix – more at -ED] : marked by having <crani*ate*>

⁴-ate \ˌāt \ *vb suffix* [ME *-aten*, fr. L *-atus*, pp. ending] : act on (in a specified way) <insul*ate*> : cause to be modified or affected by <camphor*ate*> : cause to become <activ*ate*> : furnish with <capacit*ate*>

B USING CONTEXT CLUES

Place an X in front of each correct answer. The word may be used correctly in one or both of the sentences.

1. To <u>obviate</u> a dangerous situation is to
   ___a. adjust to it.
   ___b. dispose of it or clear it away.

2. The strikers voted to <u>negotiate</u> means
   ___a. they were not willing to discuss a settlement.
   ___b. they were willing to discuss a settlement.

3. The man was <u>articulate</u> when speaking means
   ___a. he spoke distinctly.
   ___b. he was difficult to understand.

4. He was an <u>amiable</u> sort of fellow means
   ___a. he was troublesome.
   ___b. he was friendly and easy-going.

5. Emergency phone numbers should be <u>accessible</u> means
   ___a. the numbers should be easy to get to.
   ___b. the numbers should be committed to memory.

Check your answer with the Key on page 145.

C CHECKING THE MEANING

Read the words in the boxes. Choose the word that best completes the sentence under them. Write that word on the line. Then complete the next sentence by placing an X in front of the correct answer.

1. obviate | remediable

The boy's reading problems were ________________________.
This sentence means
___a. nothing would help decrease the boy's reading problems.
___b. the boy would outgrow his reading problems.
___c. the boy's reading could be helped.

2. credible | visage

The witness' account of the crime was a ____________________ one.
This sentence means
___a. the story was hard to understand.
___b. the story was believable.
___c. the story was a lie.

3. articulate | forage

In winter, some animals must ____________________ for food.
This sentence means
___a. some animals must hunt for food in the winter.
___b. some animals change their dietary habits in the winter.
___c. some animals must go without food in the winter.

4. amiable | visage

The old man's _______________________ declined with age.
This sentence means
___a. his appearance declined as he got older.
___b. his vision declined as he got older.
___c. his stamina declined as he got older.

5. forage | patronage

The storekeeper thanked his customers for their _______________________.
This sentence means
___a. he thanked his customers for paying with a credit card.
___b. he thanked his customers for using coupons.
___c. he thanked his customers for their business.

Check your answers with the Key on page 145.

SEQUENCE 9-26

D COMPLETING THE SENTENCES

Choose a word from the box that best completes each sentence. Write it on the line.

obviate	credible	articulate	accessible
forage	amiable	negotiate	remediable

1. Often, employees must ________________________ a salary increase.
2. An ____________________ person is usually very popular.
3. The road was ________________________ only to four-wheel-drive vehicles.
4. Many learning problems are _________________________.
5. He wished to ____________________ the problem at hand.

Check your answers with the Key on page 145.

E USING THE SKILL

Underline the word that best completes each sentence.

1. Wild animals must (negotiate, forage) for food and shelter.
2. A man's (visage, patronage) is very important.
3. The criminal's story was not a (amiable, credible) one.
4. The manager was happy for his customers' (obviate, patronage).
5. A small child is usually not very (articulate, obviate).

Check your answers with the Key on page 145.

F SUPPLEMENTARY WRITING EXERCISE

The suffixes that were taught in this lesson are:

-ate	-able/-ible	-age

Write sentences in which you use three of the suffixes in a word in the sentence.

1. ____
2. ____
3. ____

A WRITING THE WORDS

A. Write these words on the blank lines. Then say each word.

Write

apology	1.	____________
theology	2.	____________
anthology	3.	____________
etymology	4.	____________
dialogue	5.	____________
monologue	6.	____________
catalogue	7.	____________
synonym	8.	____________
antonym	9.	____________
pseudonym	10.	____________

B. Each word ends with a suffix. Write the suffix for each word.

1. ____________
2. ____________
3. ____________
4. ____________
5. ____________
6. ____________
7. ____________
8. ____________
9. ____________
10. ____________

THESE SUFFIXES HAVE MEANINGS RELATED TO **SPOKEN** AND **WRITTEN WORDS**.

-logue *or* **-log** \ˌlȯg, ˌläg \ *n comb form* [ME *-logue*, fr. OF, fr. L *-logus*, fr. Gk *-logos*, fr. *legein* to speak – more at LEGEND] **1** : discourse : talk <duo*logue*> **2** : student : specialist <sino*logue*>

-lo-gy \ l-ə-jē \ *n comb form* [ME *-logie*, fr. OF, fr. L *-logia*, fr. Gk, fr. *logos* word] **1** : oral or written expression <phraseo*logy*> **2** : doctrine : theory : science <ethno*logy*>

-onym \ə-ˌnim \ *n comb form* [ME, fr. L *-onymum*, fr. Gk *-ōnymon*, fr. *onyma* – more at NAME] : name : word <ant*onym*>

B USING CONTEXT CLUES

Place an X in front of each correct answer. The word may be used correctly in one or both of the sentences.

1. The little boy's apology was accepted by his mother means
   ___a. the little boy was not sorry for what he did.
   ___b. the little boy told his mother he was sorry.

2. The theme of the anthology was love and kindness means
   ___a. the collection of poems focused on love and kindness.
   ___b. the play was about love and kindness.

3. The student planned to study etymology means
   ___a. he planned to study insects.
   ___b. he planned to study word origins.

4. Every church has a theology of its own means
   ___a. each church has its own system of beliefs.
   ___b. each church has its own minister.

5. The man delivered his monologue before the delegation means
   ___a. he participated in a debate.
   ___b. he gave a speech meant to be delivered by one person.

Check your answers with the Key on page 145.

C CHECKING THE MEANING

Read the words in the boxes. Choose the word that best completes the sentence under them. Write that word on the line. Then complete the next sentence by placing an X in front of the correct answer.

1. dialogue apology

A long distance ____________________ on the telephone can be very expensive.
This sentence means
___a. a long distance conversation can be very expensive.
___b. a long distance trip can be very expensive.
___c. a telegram can be very expensive.

2. monologue catalogue

The library ____________________ is a good source of information.
This sentence means
___a. the library has many informational books.
___b. the index of all books shelved in the library is useful.
___c. the library staff is very helpful.

3. theology synonym

The teacher asked her students to find a ________________ for each word.
This sentence means
___a. she wanted her class to list words with opposite meanings.
___b. she wanted her class to list words with similar spellings.
___c. she wanted her class to list words with similar meanings.

4. antonym anthology

There is an ____________________ for almost every word in the English language.
This sentence means
___a. almost every word has a word that means its exact opposite.
___b. each word has only one acceptable meaning.
___c. a dictionary meaning exists for every word in the language.

5. pseudonym etymology

Many authors use a ____________________.
This sentence means
___a. many authors use another name in place of their own.
___b. many authors do not sign a manuscript.
___c. many authors sign their real name to their manuscripts.

Check your answers with the Key on page 145.

D COMPLETING THE SENTENCES

Choose a word from the box that best completes each sentence. Write it on the line.

apology	etymology	catalogue	monologue
dialogue	theology	synonym	anthology

1. The ____________________ was on the bestseller list for ten weeks.
2. A ____________________ involves at least two people.
3. His decision to study ____________________ required dedication and faith.
4. Many large department stores offer ____________________ shopping.
5. The student offered an ____________________ for his tardiness.

Check your answers with the Key on page 145.

E USING THE SKILL

Underline the word that best completes each sentence.

1. The actor delivered a (monologue, etymology) before the first act.
2. A (theology, synonym) is a word having a similar meaning to a given word.
3. The study of (theology, etymology) concerns word origins.
4. The actor spoke one last (monologue, catalogue) before he died.
5. A (antonym, pseudonym) is used in place of one's real name.

Check your answers with the Key on page 145.

F SUPPLEMENTARY WRITING EXERCISE

The suffixes that were taught in this lesson are:

-logy	-logue	-onym

Write sentences in which you use each of the suffixes in a word in the sentence.

1. ____
2. ____
3. ____

A WRITING THE WORDS

A. Write these words on the blank lines. Then say each word.

Write

thermometer	1.	______________
perimeter	2.	______________
chronometer	3.	______________
pedometer	4.	______________
octagon	5.	______________
pentagon	6.	______________
polygon	7.	______________
triangular	8.	______________
rectangular	9.	______________
spectacular	10.	______________

B. Each word ends with a suffix. Write the suffix for each word.

1. ______________
2. ______________
3. ______________
4. ______________
5. ______________
6. ______________
7. ______________
8. ______________
9. ______________
10. ______________

THESE SUFFIXES HAVE MEANINGS RELTED TO **MEASUREMENT** OR SHOW **RELATIONSHIP**.

-gon \ˌgän *also* -gən \ *n comb form* [NL *-gonum,* fr. Gk *-gōnon,* fr. *gōnia* angle; akin to Gk *gony* knee –more at KNEE] : figure having (so many) angles <deca*gon*>

[1]**me-ter** \ˈmēt-ər \ *n* [ME, fr. OE & MF; OE *mēter,* fr. L *metrum,* fr. Gk *metron* measure, meter; MF *metre,* fr. OF, fr. L *metrum* – more at MEASURE] **1 a** : systematically arranged and measured rhythm in verse: (1) : rhythm that continuously repeats in a single basic pattern <iambic ~ > (2) : rhythm characterized by regular recurrence of a systematic arrangement of basic patterns in larger figures <ballad ~ > **b** : a measure or unit of metrical verse – usu. used in combination and pronounced \ m-ət-ər \ <penta*meter*>; compare FOOT 4 **c** : a fixed metrical pattern : verse form **2** : the basic recurrent rhythmical pattern of note values, accents, and beats per measure in music
[2]**meter** \ˈmēt-ər \ *n* [ME, fr. *meten* to mete] : one that measures; *esp* : an official measurer of commodities
[3]**meter** \ˈmēt-ər \ *n* [F *mètre,* fr. Gk *metron* measure] : the basic metric unit of length – see METRIC SYSTEM table
[4]**meter** \ˈmēt-ər \ n [*-meter*] **1** : an instrument for measuring and sometimes recording the amount of something <a gas ~ > **2** : a philatelic cover bearing an impression of a postage meter
[5]**meter** *vt* **1** : to measure by means of a meter **2** : to supply in a measured or regulated amount **3** : to print postal indicia on by means of a postage meter
-me-ter \ mәd-ә(r), m әtә- *in some words* ˌmēt- \ *n comb form* [F *-mètre,* fr. Gk *metron* measure] : instrument or means for measuring <baro*meter*>

-u-lar \ (y) ə-lər \ *adj suffix* [L *-ularis,* fr. *-ulus, -ula, -ulum* -ule + *-aris* -ar] : of, relating to, or resembling <valv*ular*>

B USING CONTEXT CLUES

Place an X in front of each correct answer. The word may be used correctly in one or both of the sentences.

1. A pedometer was used while jogging means
   ___a. an instrument to measure was used.
   ___b. the jogger counted the distance he jogged.

2. The ship's chronometer was accurate means
   ___a. the ship's speed was accurate.
   ___b. the ship's time was accurate.

3. Establish the perimeter of the field means
   ___a. establish the boundaries of the field.
   ___b. establish the distance around the field.

4. The sail was triangular in shape means
   ___a. the sail had four sides.
   ___b. the sail had three sides.

5. The figure was a polygon means
   ___a. the figure had many sides.
   ___b. the figure had many angles.

Check your answers with the Key on page 146.

C CHECKING THE MEANING

Read the words in the boxes. Choose the word that best completes the sentence under them. Write that word on the line. Then complete the next sentence by placing an X in front of the correct answer.

1. thermometer | chronometer

A ______________________ was used to measure heat transfer in the experiment.
This sentence means
___a. an instrument used to measure distance was used in the experiment.
___b. an instrument used to measure temperature was used in the experiment.
___c. an instrument used to measure height was used in the experiment.

2. pentagon | polygon

A star is an example of a ______________________.
This sentence means
___a. a star has eight sides and angles.
___b. a star has four sides and four angles.
___c. a star has five sides and five angles.

3. octagon | rectangular

The puzzle had the shape of an ____________________.
This sentence means
___a. the puzzle had six sides to it.
___b. the puzzle had eight sides and eight angles.
___c. the puzzle was circular in shape.

4. spectacular | perimeter

The event turned out to be ________________________.
This sentence means
___a. the event was something to see.
___b. the event was one of many common events.
___c. the event was filled with things to do.

5. pedometer | rectangular

The figure was ______________________ in shape.
This sentence means
___a. the figure had four sides and four angles.
___b. the figure had five sides and five angles.
___c. the figure had six sides and six angles.

Check your answers with the Key on page 146.

D COMPLETING THE SENTENCES

Choose a word from the box that best completes each sentence. Write it on the line.

polygon	pedometer	chronometer	spectacular
pentagon	perimeter	triangular	thermometer

1. A ____________________ view can be seen from the mountaintop.
2. A ____________________ will show you how far you have walked.
3. Synchronize your ____________________ to Greenwich mean time.
4. Walk the ____________________ of the room to determine its size.
5. One of the buildings used by military personnel is _______________ in shape.

Check your answers with the Key on page 146.

E USING THE SKILL

Underline the word that best completes each sentence.

1. Her body temperature registered 98.6 on a (chronometer, thermometer).
2. The show was (rectangular, spectacular)!
3. A (polygon, pentagon) has five sides.
4. A (pedometer, chronometer) measured the distance I ran.
5. An apple turnover is (triangular, rectangular) in shape.

Check your answers with the Key on page 146.

F SUPPLEMENTARY WRITING EXERCISE

The suffixes that were taught in this lesson are:

-meter	-gon	-ular

Write sentences in which you use each of the suffixes in a word in the sentence.

1. ____
2. ____
3. ____

A WRITING THE WORDS

A. Write these words on the blank lines. Then say each word.

Write

pathetic	1.	______________
phonetic	2.	______________
prophetic	3.	______________
aesthetic	4.	______________
exotic	5.	______________
antibiotic	6.	______________
symbiotic	7.	______________
curricular	8.	______________
monocular	9.	______________
dissimilar	10.	______________

B. Each word ends with a suffix. Write the suffix for each word.

1. ______________
2. ______________
3. ______________
4. ______________
5. ______________
6. ______________
7. ______________
8. ______________
9. ______________
10. ______________

THESE SUFFIXES HAVE MEANINGS RELATED TO AN **ACTION** OR MEAN **CHARACTERISTIC OF**.

-ar \ər *also* ˌär \ *adj suffix* [ME, fr. L *-aris*, alter. of *-alis* -al] : of or relating to <molecul*ar*> : being <spectacul*ar*> : resembling <oracul*ar*>

-et-ic \ ˈet-ik \ *adj suffix* [L & Gk; L *-eticus*, fr. Gk *-etikos*, *-ētikos*, fr. *-etos*, *-ētos*, ending of certain verbals] : -IC <limn*etic*] – often in adjectives corresponding to nouns ending in *-esis* <gen*etic*>

-ot-ic \ ˈät-ik \ *adj suffix* [Gk *-ōtikos*, fr. *-ōtos*, ending of verbals, fr. *-o-* (stem of causative verbs in *-oun*) + *tos*, suffix forming verbals – more at -ED] **1 a** : of, relating to, or characterized by a (specified) action, process, or condition <symbi*otic*> **b** : having an abnormal or diseased condition of a (specified) kind <epizo*otic*> **2** : showing an increase or a formation of <leukocyt*otic*>

B USING CONTEXT CLUES

Place an X in front of each correct answer. The word may be used correctly in one or both of the sentences.

1. The street child was <u>pathetic</u> means
   ___a. one could feel glad for the child.
   ___b. one could feel sad for the child.

2. A <u>phonetic</u> transcription is one that
   ___a. is made by the way words look.
   ___b. is made by the way words sound.

3. A <u>symbiotic</u> relationship is a relationship
   ___a. that is mutually advantageous.
   ___b. where mutual support is given.

4. The <u>curricular</u> activities are necessary in a school means
   ___a. the prescribed course of study is necessary.
   ___b. football and basketball are necessary.

5. A person that has <u>monocular</u> vision has
   ___a. vision in two eyes.
   ___b. vision in one eye.

Check your answers with the Key on page 146.

C CHECKING THE MEANING

Read the words in the boxes. Choose the word that best completes the sentence under them. Write that word on the line. Then complete the next sentence by placing an X in front of the correct answer.

1. phonetic | aesthetic

An artist deals in ________________________ values.
This sentence means
___a. an artist deals with the nature of color.
___b. an artist deals with the nature of beauty.
___c. an artist deals with the nature of design.

2. prophetic | antibiotic

An ________________________ is given to destroy harmful microbes.
This sentence means
___a. a substance used to combat disease is given.
___b. a substance used to help germs grow is given.
___c. a substance used to help heal an injury is given.

3. exotic | pathetic

At one time, the potato was considered an ____________________ plant.
This sentence means
___a. at one time the potato was considered a natural plant.
___b. at one time the potato was considered an unusual plant.
___c. at one time the potato was very popular.

4. dissimilar | curricular

The two metals had ________________________ characteristics.
This sentence means
___a. the two metals were alike.
___b. the two metals were almost alike.
___c. the two metals were not alike.

5. monocular | symbiotic

The insects were ________________________.
This sentence means
___a. the insects were dissimilar.
___b. the insects were similar.
___c. the insects were mutually beneficial to each other.

Check your answers with the Key on page 146.

D COMPLETING THE SENTENCES

Choose a word from the box that best completes each sentence. Write it on the line.

pathetic	prophetic	exotic	monocular
phonetic	curricular	aesthetic	antibiotic

1. A cat in the rain is a ______________________________ sight.
2. The ___________________________ offerings of the school were varied.
3. A Venus Fly Trap is an example of an ________________________ plant.
4. The pianist had an _____________________________ nature.
5. The ____________________________ alphabet is used in speech therapy.

Check your answers with the Key on page 146.

E USING THE SKILL

Underline the word that best completes each sentence.

1. The man's warnings about a disaster were (prophetic, symbiotic).
2. A statue may prove to be (prophetic, aesthetic) to those who like art.
3. The two courses were (curricular, dissimilar) in content.
4. The cat and dog enjoyed a (symbiotic, phonetic) existence.
5. The (antibiotic, symbiotic) cured the man's infection.

Check your answers with the Key on page 146.

F SUPPLEMENTARY WRITING EXERCISE

The suffixes that were taught in this lesson are:

-etic	-otic	-ar

Write sentences in which you use each of the suffixes in a word in the sentence.

1. ____
2. ____
3. ____

A WRITING THE WORDS

A. Write these words on the blank lines.
Then say each word.

		Write
decade	1.	______________
barricade	2.	______________
serenade	3.	______________
devilish	4.	______________
brackish	5.	______________
brandish	6.	______________
prosthesis	7.	______________
analysis	8.	______________
emphasis	9.	______________
osmosis	10.	______________

B. Each word ends with a suffix. Write the suffix for each word.

1. ______________
2. ______________
3. ______________
4. ______________
5. ______________
6. ______________
7. ______________
8. ______________
9. ______________
10. ______________

THESE SUFFIXES HAVE MEANINGS RELATED TO AN **ACTION** OR MEAN **CHARACTERISITC OF**.

SEQUENCE 9-30

-ade \ ād \ *n suffix* [ME, fr. MF, fr. Oprov *-ada*, fr. LL *-ata*, fr. L, fem. of *-atus* -ate] **1** : act : action <block*ade*> **2** : product; *esp* : sweet drink <lemon*ade*>

-ish \ ish \ *adj suffix* [ME, fr. OE *-isc*; akin to OHG *-isc*, ish, Gk *-iskos*, dim. suffix] **1** : of, relating to, or being – chiefly in adjectives indicating nationality or ethnic group <Finn*ish*> **2 a** : characteristic of <boy*ish*> <mul*ish*> **b** : inclined or liable to <book*ish*> <qualm*ish*> **c** (1) : having a touch or trace of <summer*ish*> : somewhat <purpl*ish*> (2) : having the approximate age of <forty*ish*> (3) : being or occurring at the approximate time of <eight*ish*>

-sis \ səs \ *n suffix*, *pl* **-ses** \ ˌsēz \ [L, fr. Gk, fem. suffix of action] : process : action <peristal*sis*>

B USING CONTEXT CLUES

Place an X in front of each correct answer. The word may be used correctly in one or both of the sentences.

1. A barricade was erected across the road means
   ___a. a road was cleared to provide an escape route.
   ___b. an obstruction was put across the road.

2. A decade is equal to
   ___a. twenty years.
   ___b. ten years.

3. An analysis was made of the problem means
   ___a. the problem was broken into separate parts.
   ___b. the problem was considered as a whole.

4. A prosthesis was used to replace the man's missing arm means
   ___a. the arm became part of his body.
   ___b. the replaced arm was artificial.

5. Water may pass through the cell wall by osmosis means
   ___a. water may be absorbed by the cell wall.
   ___b. water may be cast off by the cell wall.

Check your answers with the Key on page 146.

C CHECKING THE MEANING

Read the words in the boxes. Choose the word that best completes the sentence under them. Write that word on the line. Then complete the next sentence by placing an X in front of the correct answer.

1. | serenade | | decade |

A ________________________ can quiet a noisy crowd.
This sentence means
___a. music can quiet a crowd.
___b. a stringed instrument can quiet a crowd.
___c. a musician can make a crowd quiet.

2. | brackish | | brandish |

Water in Lake Pontchartrain is __________________________.
This sentence means
___a. the water is fresh water.
___b. the water is dirty.
___c. the water is a little salty.

3. | devilish | | brandish |

I saw the native ___________________________ his spear at the white men.
This sentence means
___a. the native threw his spear at the white men.
___b. the native shook his spear at the white men.
___c. the native threw away his spear.

4. | emphasis | | analysis |

Special _______________________ must be placed on homework.
This sentence means
___a. less importance must be given to homework.
___b. no importance must be given to homework.
___c. special importance must be given to homework.

5. | prosthesis | | osmosis |

A _________________________ replaces a missing limb.
This sentence means
___a. an artificial part cannot correct a defect.
___b. an artificial part can create beauty.
___c. an artificial part can help correct a defect.

Check your answers with the Key on page 146.

D COMPLETING THE SENTENCES

Choose a word from the box that best completes each sentence. Write it on the line.

barricade	brackish	devilish	emphasis
decade	brandish	analysis	osmosis

1. Another ____________________ might pass before man travels to Mars.

2. The ____________________ water was not good to drink.

3. The boy had a ____________________ gleam in his eye.

4. The complex problem needed much ____________________.

5. One must place ____________________ on good behavior.

Check your answers with the Key on page 146.

E USING THE SKILL

Underline the word that best completes each sentence.

1. The soldiers erected a (serenade, barricade) to keep the enemy at bay.

2. A (devilish, brackish) visage on a child may cause his parents concern.

3. One cannot place enough (prosthesis, emphasis) on honesty.

4. I saw the man (brackish, brandish) a club at the growling dog.

5. The (decade, barricade) proved to be a strong defense.

Check your answers with the Key on page 146.

F SUPPLEMENTARY WRITING EXERCISE

The suffixes that were taught in this lesson are:

-ade	-ish	-sis

Write sentences in which you use each of the suffixes in a word in the sentence.

1. ____

2. ____

3. ____

G SENTENCES FOR SPELLING EXERCISE

SEQUENCE 9-1

1. The play required that the actor learn a complicated monologue.
2. The great stone monolith was dedicated to war veterans.
3. Many people feel monogamy is the only correct marital agreement.
4. The child always drew monochromatic pictures.
5. A jury must be free of biased opinions.
6. The wealthy family took biannual cruises to Greece.
7. A carrot is a type of biennial plant.
8. The triangle is a very common geometric figure.
9. The state fair was a triennial event.
10. A triarchy is not a common form of government.

G SENTENCES FOR SPELLING EXERCISE

SEQUENCE 9-2

1. In the United States, Presidential elections are held on a quadrennial basis.
2. A quadrant is an instrument used to measure altitude.
3. A quadrilateral is one type of geometric figure.
4. A quadruped is a four-footed animal.
5. A pentagon always has five sides and five angles.
6. An athletic competition with five events is called a pentathlon.
7. A true insect is a hexapod.
8. A pentarchy has five leaders.
9. A hexagon always has six sides.
10. The poet used hexameter to write his lines of poetry.

G SENTENCES FOR SPELLING EXERCISE

SEQUENCE 9-3

1. According to the Roman calendar, <u>September</u> is the seventh month.
2. A <u>septennial</u> event is held every seven years.
3. The musical composition was performed by a <u>septet</u> of musicians.
4. Many commercial signs are <u>octagon</u> in shape.
5. An <u>octopus</u> has eight tentacles.
6. The music was written one <u>octave</u> higher than the girl could sing.
7. An <u>octet</u> is a composition written for eight instruments.
8. The metric system is a <u>decimal</u> system.
9. A <u>decimeter</u> is a measurement of length.
10. Tornadoes often <u>decimate</u> neighborhoods.

G SENTENCES FOR SPELLING EXERCISE

SEQUENCE 9-4

1. <u>Polytheist</u> theories stress the concept of more than one God.
2. A <u>miscreant</u> is one who behaves criminally.
3. Many people find it difficult to accept <u>miscegenation</u>.
4. Many communes support <u>polygamous</u> relationships.
5. A <u>philanthropist</u> shows genuine concern for humanity.
6. Many charitable organizations appeal to <u>philanthropy</u>.
7. The <u>philatelist</u> owned a valuable collection of international stamps.
8. The man's actions express a true <u>misogyny</u>.
9. After a series of broken marriages, the man became a <u>misogamist</u>.
10. Following the war, the veteran became a <u>misanthropist</u>.

G SENTENCES FOR SPELLING EXERCISE

SEQUENCE 9-5

1. The microcosm was accurate to the smallest detail.
2. The astronomer used a micrometer to measure distance on his charts.
3. Most human beings are not apodal.
4. The scientist isolated the microbe responsible for the disease.
5. An apologue stresses a moral value of some kind.
6. The astronomer measured the perigee of the planet.
7. The apogee of the mountain range was 15,000 feet.
8. The agency stored much of its material on microfilm.
9. The perimeter of the square is equal to four times the length of one side.
10. The periphery of the estate was protected by an elaborate security system.

G SENTENCES FOR SPELLING EXERCISE

SEQUENCE 9-6

1. The cream will coagulate and become cottage cheese.
2. We will not coerce you into doing the task.
3. Your comment was cogent and should be examined.
4. The sentences in the paragraph cohere.
5. Complete symmetry is difficult to achieve.
6. We can extend sympathy for one in sorrow.
7. The symposium was concerned with the city's problems.
8. An autograph is a personal expression.
9. An autocrat rules with absolute power.
10. A self-employed person has complete autonomy.

G SENTENCES FOR SPELLING EXERCISE

SEQUENCE 9-7

1. Use a <u>diagram</u> to explain the problem.
2. A doctor can <u>diagnose</u> many diseases.
3. The debaters were engaged in <u>dialogue</u> for more than two hours.
4. The jury tried to <u>discern</u> if the defendant was telling the truth.
5. The city will <u>disburse</u> additional school funds next week.
6. Use <u>discretion</u> when you hear a rumor.
7. An apothecary is licensed to <u>dispense</u> medication.
8. Some flowers are <u>perennial</u>; others are annual.
9. The odor of frying bacon seemed to <u>permeate</u> the campsite.
10. The man told the judge he did not <u>perpetrate</u> the crime.

G SENTENCES FOR SPELLING EXERCISE

SEQUENCE 9-8

1. The suspect remained <u>adamant</u> that he did not perpetrate the crime.
2. Exercise is a necessary <u>adjunct</u> to food and sleep to maintain a healthy body.
3. The football field is <u>adjacent</u> to the field house.
4. The king will <u>abdicate</u> his throne for the woman he loves.
5. The <u>abolition</u> of slavery in the United States occurred in 1865.
6. A teacher will often <u>abridge</u> textbook material.
7. New laws <u>abrogate</u> old laws.
8. An <u>obese</u> person must learn to change his poor eating habits.
9. Nuclear energy has the potential to <u>obliterate</u> all evidence of life.
10. The computer has made the typewriter <u>obsolete</u>.

G SENTENCES FOR SPELLING EXERCISE

SEQUENCE 9-9

1. A series of facts will help you deduce a solution to the mystery.
2. The process of dehydration eliminates moisture.
3. The man asked his wife to delineate their vacation plans.
4. I read an excerpt from the book in a magazine.
5. "The Man Without a Country" is the story of an expatriate.
6. The most expedient way to the ballpark is a shortcut through the woods.
7. Telling the truth will help expiate your guilty conscience.
8. Afraid to take the exam, the girl used subterfuge by feigning a headache.
9. The Bill of Rights does not subjugate the American people.
10. An employee is subordinate to his employer.

G SENTENCES FOR SPELLING EXERCISE

SEQUENCE 9-10

1. All officers on a military base must synchronize their watches.
2. A synopsis of the new play can be found in today's newspaper.
3. The important news story will be given to the newspaper syndicate.
4. A worker hopes to earn wages commensurate with his ability.
5. Some individuals commune better with nature than with people.
6. Under communism, all property is owned by the state.
7. Your compassion for sick animals is admirable.
8. The loser in the election will concede on national television.
9. Much expertise is needed to conciliate a peace between the countries.
10. A parent should not condone a child's poor behavior.

G SENTENCES FOR SPELLING EXERCISE

SEQUENCE 9-11

1. A person's binocular vision should be tested annually.
2. The oculist gave the boy a thorough eye examination.
3. An optician will fill your eyeglass prescription.
4. Damage to the optic nerve can result in a loss of eyesight.
5. A monocle is an eyeglass that covers only one eye.
6. The holiday parade was a brilliant spectacle.
7. Many people are circumspect in the way that they deal with strangers.
8. The hotel manager will inspect the rooms for cleanliness.
9. Legend has it that a specter lives inside the old mansion.
10. Due to his unruly behavior, the spectator was asked to leave the stadium.

G SENTENCES FOR SPELLING EXERCISE

SEQUENCE 9-12

1. A high school education will benefit the recipient.
2. The decision to adjourn the meeting was a unanimous one.
3. Because of its amatory content, the book was removed from the school's library.
4. The politician was able to animate the crowds with his speeches.
5. The church was well known for its many benevolent deeds.
6. The relationship between the two foreign powers was an amicable one.
7. The amorous relationship between the two was short lived.
8. A benediction was given at the end of each school assembly.
9. The girl was popular because she was very amiable.
10. There was great animosity between brother and sister.

G SENTENCES FOR SPELLING EXERCISE

SEQUENCE 9-13

1. The rooms in the mansion were very capacious.
2. By coincidence, the two girls had the same first and last name.
3. The accident resulted in severe injuries to the cars' occupants.
4. Attempts to capture the escaped prisoner were futile.
5. Circumstances surrounding the incident were vague.
6. Cartoons are known for their ability to captivate a child's attention.
7. The teacher felt that all her students were capable of passing the test.
8. The story the boy told about flying saucers was hardly credible.
9. Never give much credence to idle gossip.
10. Job applicants were asked to submit their credentials in person.

G SENTENCES FOR SPELLING EXERCISE

SEQUENCE 9-14

1. A corpulent person has a good chance of suffering a heart attack.
2. In order to be genuine, an antique must be over 100 years old.
3. A cordial person usually has many friends.
4. The relationship shared by the two men was a congenial one.
5. A cell that is found in the blood is called a corpuscle.
6. The criminal turned himself in of his own accord.
7. Discord in a marriage often leads to divorce.
8. A nurse will attend to a patient's corporeal needs.
9. The oldest progenitor in our family sailed on the Mayflower.
10. The politician used campaign promises to generate more votes.

G SENTENCES FOR SPELLING EXERCISE

SEQUENCE 9-15

1. A young child is often impetuous in his actions.
2. The attempt to implement the new rules was unsuccessful.
3. Careless use of gasoline will deplete the supply.
4. The decorator chose furnishings to complement the décor.
5. The magazine was added as a supplement to the newspaper.
6. To recall a political candidate, a petition must be circulated.
7. The firm was looking for an intelligent and competent accountant.
8. Parents must admonish their children when necessary.
9. A classroom monitor helps discipline the class while the teacher is gone.
10. A premonition can serve as a forewarning.

G SENTENCES FOR SPELLING EXERCISE

SEQUENCE 9-16

1. The newlyweds are living in a duplex by the lake.
2. The duplex was located in an apartment complex.
3. The additional information changed the complexion of the problem.
4. The bank will make a duplicate of your monthly statement.
5. A question at the wrong time may complicate a problem.
6. Possession of the document may implicate you in the case.
7. The biologist tried to replicate life in a test tube.
8. The director wants an explicit accounting of all money expended.
9. There was an implicit warning on the prescription bottle.
10. You are implicated in the crime because of your complicity.

G SENTENCES FOR SPELLING EXERCISE

SEQUENCE 9-17

1. Most people work for tangible rewards.
2. The school was tangent to our home.
3. There was a tangle in the fisherman's line.
4. Foreign relations are based on knowledge and tact.
5. The blind rely upon their tactile skills to get around.
6. Continuity is achieved when people show up for work every day.
7. A tenant farmer receives only one half of his crop.
8. Animals become tenacious when they fight to protect their young.
9. Most people have a tendency to be honest and fair about matters.
10. A basic tenet of life to live by is honesty.

G SENTENCES FOR SPELLING EXERCISE

SEQUENCE 9-18

1. In clear weather, a pilot will use visual landing markers.
2. The use of television in education is on the rise.
3. The program made evident what the audience had suspected.
4. Congress sets aside land to help preserve the wilderness.
5. The city reservoir was completely dry.
6. Many early Americans were placed on a reservation for their own safety.
7. The inscription on the watch was very sentimental.
8. A complete description of the fugitive was broadcast on radio and television.
9. The disc jockey played a transcription of the commercial.
10. A nurse cannot write a prescription for drugs.

G SENTENCES FOR SPELLING EXERCISE

SEQUENCE 9-19

1. Club members will <u>convene</u> at 10:00 a.m. to discuss grievances.
2. Solar energy may become the next <u>convenience</u> for modern man.
3. A constitutional <u>convention</u> was held to ratify the new document.
4. Many stores sell a <u>conversion</u> kit for creating a custom car.
5. The problem was corrected by a <u>reversion</u> to the former schedule.
6. An <u>inversion</u> of the elements in the gas heater was approved.
7. Please clean the <u>obverse</u> side of the plate.
8. A chance remark may <u>provoke</u> an argument.
9. To <u>revoke</u> a law is to change the status of the law by legal action.
10. Most religions <u>invoke</u> a blessing at the end of their services.

G SENTENCES FOR SPELLING EXERCISE

SEQUENCE 9-20

1. The doctor attempted to <u>elucidate</u> the man's illness as simply as possible.
2. The sun screens on the windows were <u>translucent</u>.
3. The congressional committee voted to <u>revive</u> some outdated laws.
4. The colors on the television set were extremely <u>vivid</u>.
5. Due to her <u>vivacious</u> personality, the little girl made friends easily.
6. A burning log in a fireplace is a <u>luminous</u> object.
7. The sun is a <u>luminary</u>.
8. The man used his headlights to <u>illuminate</u> the dark roadway.
9. Many traditional holidays and celebrations are <u>convivial</u> events.
10. The lawyer attempted to present a <u>lucid</u> argument to the jury.

G SENTENCES FOR SPELLING EXERCISE — SEQUENCE 9-21

1. The betrayal of the man by his girlfriend caused their breakup.
2. The denial of God's existence is called atheism.
3. The refusal to aid people in distress frequently results in crisis.
4. The king chose abdication so he would be able to marry a commoner.
5. The abduction of the Lindberg baby drew nationwide attention.
6. The calculation made by the mathematician was erroneous.
7. The dissimilarity of cultures caused frequent conflicts between the two nations.
8. There is much disparity between the income of the rich and the income of the poor.
9. The diversity of cultures within the country created unique problems.
10. Applicants sometimes lie to meet eligibility requirements.

G SENTENCES FOR SPELLING EXERCISE — SEQUENCE 9-22

1. The photographer set the wrong exposure and ruined the film.
2. The mountain climber fell into a fissure while crossing the glacier.
3. The king chose to immure his opponents.
4. Radical groups frequently choose reactionary tactics to gain attention.
5. The recently captured eagle was placed in an aviary.
6. The beneficiary received $100,000 after the death of his uncle.
7. The pianist attended the conservatory to improve his skills.
8. The astronomer spent the evening in the observatory.
9. The nightclub performer had a large repertory of songs.
10. The depository for nuclear weapons is heavily guarded.

G SENTENCES FOR SPELLING EXERCISE

SEQUENCE 9-23

1. Long ago, a physical <u>abnormality</u> would often result in death.
2. An old quotation states that "<u>familiarity</u> breeds contempt."
3. The man was known for his <u>geniality</u>.
4. Man has a difficult time grasping the concept of <u>infinity</u>.
5. The ruptured gas line filled the air with a <u>malodorous</u> smell.
6. The <u>melodious</u> strains of the music lulled the baby to sleep.
7. The tank was <u>impervious</u> to the enemy's weapons.
8. The <u>contrariness</u> of the brothers resulted in numerous fights.
9. The <u>aggressiveness</u> of the German nation helped launch World War II.
10. Show people are known for the <u>tawdriness</u> of their dress.

G SENTENCES FOR SPELLING EXERCISE

SEQUENCE 9-24

1. Many animals are <u>nocturnal</u>.
2. A public library provides a <u>communal</u> service.
3. Land <u>marginal</u> to a desert would be difficult to farm.
4. The producer wanted the characters to act in a <u>natural</u> way.
5. As they grow old, people often become <u>senile</u>.
6. A <u>projectile</u> was launched toward the moon.
7. The husband and wife were not able to <u>reconcile</u> their differences.
8. A strange <u>asteroid</u> was seen revolving around the sun.
9. The psychiatrist tried to help the <u>paranoid</u> man overcome his illness.
10. A <u>spheroid</u> object will often bounce.

G SENTENCES FOR SPELLING EXERCISE

SEQUENCE 9-25

1. The obese man was placed on a restrictive diet.
2. The runner's objective was to beat the competition.
3. Consider all the facts in order to prevent making a subjective decision.
4. A handshake is used to signify friendship.
5. The accountant admitted his error in calculation and wanted to rectify it.
6. Congress voted to nullify the tariff on imports.
7. The chemist attempted to neutralize the corrosive effect of the acid.
8. The cocktail party gave the employees a chance to fraternize.
9. Many people objected to the attempts to nationalize all industry.
10. Attempts by the corporation to monopolize the industry failed.

G SENTENCES FOR SPELLING EXERCISE

SEQUENCE 9-26

1. He wished to obviate all facts concerning the trial.
2. The opposing sides felt they were ready to negotiate.
3. The disc jockey had an amiable voice.
4. The island was only accessible by airplane.
5. The teacher felt the boy's problem was a remediable one.
6. The student became very articulate in a debate.
7. The defendant told a credible story.
8. The soldiers had to forage for their food.
9. His visage was controlled in spite of his anger.
10. Merchants appreciate steady patronage.

G SENTENCES FOR SPELLING EXERCISE

SEQUENCE 9-27

1. The girl owed her teacher an <u>apology</u>.
2. The poet's first <u>anthology</u> would soon be available in bookstores.
3. The study of <u>etymology</u> can help clarify word meanings.
4. Upon graduation, the young man planned to major in <u>theology</u>
5. A <u>monologue</u> is meant to be delivered by a single person.
6. The <u>dialogue</u> between the two politicians was very heated.
7. The <u>catalogue</u> listed all the merchandise sold in the department store.
8. A <u>thesaurus</u> is a good source for finding a synonym for a word.
9. An <u>antonym</u> is a word that means the opposite of another word.
10. The author chose to use a <u>pseudonym</u>.

G SENTENCES FOR SPELLING EXERCISE

SEQUENCE 9-28

1. The use of a <u>pedometer</u> will measure the distance you've walked.
2. A person's temperature is taken with a <u>thermometer</u>.
3. A <u>chronometer</u> is a necessary part of a ship's controls.
4. The distance around a square is known as its <u>perimeter</u>.
5. A <u>pentagon</u> has five sides and five angles.
6. The figure represented a <u>polygon</u>.
7. The tower room was in the shape of an <u>octagon</u>.
8. The <u>triangular</u>-shaped piece of material became a dress.
9. The field was <u>rectangular</u> in shape.
10. The celebration began with a <u>spectacular</u> display of fireworks.

G SENTENCES FOR SPELLING EXERCISE — SEQUENCE 9-29

1. The hobo was a very <u>pathetic</u> sight.
2. Linguists sometimes transcribe English into the <u>phonetic</u> alphabet.
3. The <u>aesthetic</u> qualities of the design were studied carefully.
4. It was <u>prophetic</u> that he predicted the earthquake.
5. The two animals shared a <u>symbiotic</u> relationship.
6. An <u>antibiotic</u> was used to combat the girl's disease.
7. There are many <u>exotic</u> plants found in the jungle.
8. The identical twins displayed <u>dissimilar</u> personalities.
9. The <u>curricular</u> offerings of the school were quite extensive.
10. The telescope has a <u>monocular</u> eyepiece.

G SENTENCES FOR SPELLING EXERCISE — SEQUENCE 9-30

1. A <u>barricade</u> was erected to keep wild animals from entering the picnic area.
2. The couple have been married for more than a <u>decade</u>.
3. A strolling quartet will <u>serenade</u> you at the restaurant.
4. Certain fish thrive in <u>brackish</u> waters.
5. An irate person may <u>brandish</u> a club to deter further conflict.
6. The young child had a <u>devilish</u> nature.
7. It took a great deal of <u>analysis</u> to come up with a solution to the problem.
8. A <u>prosthesis</u> was necessary to take the place of the man's missing leg.
9. The school placed much <u>emphasis</u> upon students' attendance.
10. Water will pass through some materials by the process of <u>osmosis</u>.

ANSWER KEY

Sequences 9-1 to 9-3

SEQUENCE 9-1

B (page 2)

1. b
2. b
3. a
4. b
5. b

C (page 3)

1. biannual, b
2. biennial, a
3. triarchy, a
4. triennial, c
5. triangle, a

D (page 4)

1. biased
2. monologue
3. monochromatic
4. monolith
5. monogamy

E (page 4)

1. triarchy
2. biannual
3. biennial
4. triangle
5. triennial

SEQUENCE 9-2

B (page 6)

1. a
2. b
3. b
4. a
5. a

C (page 7)

1. pentarchy, c
2. hexagon, b
3. pentathlon, c
4. hexameter, a
5. hexapod, b

D (page 8)

1. quadruped
2. hexameter
3. quadrennial
4. pentagon
5. quadrant

E (page 8)

1. pentarchy
2. quadrilateral
3. hexapod
4. pentathlon
5. pentagon

SEQUENCE 9-3

B (page 10)

1. b
2. b
3. a
4. a
5. b

C (page 11)

1. octave, c
2. September, a
3. decimal, b
4. decimeter, c
5. decimate, c

D (page 12)

1. octave
2. octopus
3. octagon
4. septennial
5. September

E (page 12)

1. septet
2. decimal
3. decimeter
4. decimate
5. octet

ANSWER KEY

Sequences 9-4 to 9-6

SEQUENCE 9-4

B (page 14)

1. a
2. b
3. a
4. b
5. b

C (page 15)

1. polytheist, a
2. misogamist, b
3. miscreant, c
4. miscegenation, b
5. polygamous, a

D (page 16)

1. philanthropist
2. philanthropy
3. misogamist
4. miscreant
5. philatelist

E (page 16)

1. misanthropist
2. miscegenation
3. misogyny
4. polytheist
5. polygamous

SEQUENCE 9-5

B (page 18)

1. b
2. b
3. b
4. a
5. a

C (page 19)

1. microcosm, a
2. perimeter, c
3. periphery, c
4. perigee, a
5. microfilm, b

D (page 20)

1. apodal
2. microbe
3. apologue
4. micrometer
5. apogee

E (page 20)

1. microfilm
2. microcosm
3. perimeter
4. periphery
5. perigee

SEQUENCE 9-6

B (page 22)

1. b
2. a
3. b
4. a, b
5. a

C (page 23)

1. cogent, b
2. coerce, c
3. symposium, b
4. autocrat, c
5. autonomy, c

D (page 24)

1. coerce
2. cogent
3. cohere
4. autonomy
5. symmetry

E (page 24)

1. coagulate
2. cohere
3. autograph
4. sympathy
5. autonomy

ANSWER KEY

Sequences 9-7 to 9-9

SEQUENCE 9-7

B (page 26)

1. a
2. a
3. a
4. b
5. b

C (page 27)

1. permeate, c
2. discern, a
3. discretion, b
4. disburse, c
5. diagnose, a

D (page 28)

1. diagnose
2. discern
3. discretion
4. perennial
5. dispense

E (page 28)

1. diagram
2. permeate
3. dispense
4. dialogue
5. perpetrate

SEQUENCE 9-8

B (page 30)

1. b
2. b
3. b
4. b
5. a

C (page 31)

1. obsolete, c
2. abridge, b
3. abolition, c
4. adjunct, a
5. obliterate, b

D (page 32)

1. obsolete
2. adjacent
3. obese
4. abrogate
5. abridge

E (page 32)

1. adamant
2. abdicate
3. abrogate
4. obliterate
5. adjunct

SEQUENCE 9-9

B (page 34)

1. a, b
2. a, b
3. b
4. a
5. a

C (page 35)

1. dehydration, b
2. excerpt, a
3. deduce, b
4. subterfuge, a
5. subjugate, c

D (page 36)

1. subordinate
2. expedient
3. delineate
4. subterfuge
5. dehydration

E (page 36)

1. deduce
2. expatriate
3. subterfuge
4. delineate
5. excerpt

ANSWER KEY

Sequences 9-10 to 9-12

SEQUENCE 9-10

B (page 38)

1. b
2. b
3. a, b
4. b
5. b

C (page 39)

1. synopsis, c
2. commune, b
3. communism, a
4. condone, c
5. conciliate, c

D (page 40)

1. commensurate
2. concede
3. conciliate
4. synchronize
5. condone

E (page 40)

1. synchronize
2. commune
3. compassion
4. condone
5. synopsis

SEQUENCE 9-11

B (page 42)

1. a
2. b
3. a
4. b
5. b

C (page 43)

1. binocular, a
2. oculist, a
3. optician, c
4. optic, c
5. monocle, a

D (page 44)

1. spectacle
2. optic
3. specter
4. inspect
5. optician

E (page 44)

1. monocle
2. oculist
3. binocular
4. spectator
5. circumspect

SEQUENCE 9-12

B (page 46)

1. b
2. b
3. a
4. a
5. a

C (page 47)

1. animosity, c
2. unanimous, a
3. benevolent, c
4. benefit, c
5. benediction, b

D (page 48)

1. benevolent
2. amiable
3. amorous
4. unanimous
5. amicable

E (page 48)

1. amatory
2. animosity
3. benefit
4. benediction
5. animate

ANSWER KEY

Sequences 9-13 to 9-15

SEQUENCE 9-13

B (page 50)

1. b
2. a
3. a
4. b
5. a

C (page 51)

1. credible, c
2. credentials, b
3. capacious, a
4. credence, c
5. coincidence, b

D (page 52)

1. coincidence
2. accident
3. capture
4. capable
5. captivate

E (page 52)

1. capacious
2. credence
3. credentials
4. incident
5. credible

SEQUENCE 9-14

B (page 54)

1. a
2. b
3. a
4. b
5. a

C (page 55)

1. progenitor, a
2. genuine, b
3. congenial, a
4. corporeal, a
5. generate, c

D (page 56)

1. corpulent
2. genuine
3. cordial
4. congenial
5. corpuscle

E (page 56)

1. accord
2. discord
3. corporeal
4. progenitor
5. generate

SEQUENCE 9-15

B (page 58)

1. b
2. b
3. a
4. a
5. a

C (page 59)

1. impetuous, a
2. implement, b
3. deplete, a
4. complement, c
5. supplement, b

D (page 60)

1. deplete
2. implement
3. petition
4. impetuous
5. competent

E (page 60)

1. monitor
2. premonition
3. admonish
4. supplement
5. complement

ANSWER KEY

Sequences 9-16 to 9-18

SEQUENCE 9-16

B (page 62)

1. b
2. b
3. a, b
4. b
5. b

C (page 63)

1. complex, c
2. implicate, c
3. complicity, a
4. replicate, c
5. explicit, c

D (page 64)

1. duplicate
2. complexion
3. explicit
4. implicate
5. complicity

E (page 64)

1. complex
2. implicate
3. replicate
4. explicit
5. duplicate

SEQUENCE 9-17

B (page 66)

1. b
2. a
3. a, b
4. b
5. a, b

C (page 67)

1. tangent, a
2. tact, b
3. tangle, a
4. tenacious, c
5. tenet, a

D (page 68)

1. tangible
2. tenant
3. tenacious
4. tendency
5. tactile

E (page 68)

1. tangent
2. tact
3. tenacious
4. tendency
5. tenant

SEQUENCE 9-18

B (page 70)

1. b
2. a, b
3. b
4. a
5. a

C (page 71)

1. visual, c
2. preserve, b
3. reservoir, a
4. prescription, c
5. transcription, c

D (page 72)

1. description
2. preserve
3. transcription
4. visual
5. inscription

E (page 72)

1. reservoir
2. description
3. prescription
4. advisor
5. visual

ANSWER KEY

Sequences 9-19 to 9-21

SEQUENCE 9-19

B (page 74)

1. b
2. a, b
3. b
4. b
5. b

C (page 75)

1. convenience, b
2. convention, c
3. inversion, c
4. obverse, b
5. revoke, c

D (page 76)

1. convene
2. reversion
3. inversion
4. revoke
5. provoke

E (page 76)

1. convention
2. conversion
3. obverse
4. revoke
5. convenience

SEQUENCE 9-20

B (page 78)

1. a
2. a
3. b
4. b
5. a

C (page 79)

1. elucidate, b
2. luminary, a
3. illuminate, c
4. luminous, b
5. translucent, a

D (page 80)

1. vivacious
2. lucid
3. convivial
4. revive
5. vivid

E (page 80)

1. translucent
2. illuminate
3. luminous
4. elucidate
5. luminous

SEQUENCE 9-21

B (page 82)

1. a
2. b
3. b
4. a
5. a

C (page 83)

1. calculation, b
2. disparity, a
3. eligibility, c
4. diversity, a
5. dissimilarity, a

D (page 84)

1. abdication
2. calculation
3. abduction
4. refusal
5. betrayal

E (page 84)

1. disparity
2. diversity
3. dissimilarity
4. denial
5. eligibility

ANSWER KEY

Sequences 9-22 to 9-24

SEQUENCE 9-22

B (page 86)

1. b
2. b
3. a
4. a
5. b

C (page 87)

1. depository, b
2. repertory, a
3. observatory, a
4. conservatory, a
5. beneficiary, c

D (page 88)

1. immure
2. observatory
3. aviary
4. beneficiary
5. fissure

E (page 88)

1. exposure
2. fissure
3. reactionary
4. repertory
5. depository

SEQUENCE 9-23

B (page 90)

1. a
2. a
3. b
4. b
5. a

C (page 91)

1. melodious, c
2. aggressiveness, a
3. contrariness, c
4. tawdriness, c
5. impervious, b

D (page 92)

1. familiarity
2. impervious
3. geniality
4. infinity
5. abnormality

E (page 92)

1. melodious
2. contrariness
3. aggressiveness
4. tawdriness
5. malodorous

SEQUENCE 9-24

B (page 94)

1. b
2. b
3. b
4. a
5. a

C (page 95)

1. projectile, a
2. reconcile, c
3. asteroid, b
4. paranoid, b
5. spheroid, c

D (page 96)

1. communal
2. marginal
3. senile
4. natural
5. nocturnal

E (page 96)

1. projectile
2. asteroid
3. spheroid
4. paranoid
5. reconcile

ANSWER KEY

Sequences 9-25 to 9-27

SEQUENCE 9-25

B (page 98)

1. b
2. a
3. a
4. a
5. b

C (page 99)

1. fraternize, a
2. monopolize, c
3. neutralize, c
4. nullify, b
5. nationalize, b

D (page 100)

1. objective
2. fraternize
3. nullify
4. nationalize
5. neutralize

E (page 100)

1. restrictive
2. signify
3. rectify
4. nullify
5. subjective

SEQUENCE 9-26

B (page 102)

1. b
2. b
3. a
4. b
5. a

C (page 103)

1. remediable, c
2. credible, b
3. forage, a
4. visage, a
5. patronage, c

D (page 104)

1. negotiate
2. amiable
3. accessible
4. remediable
5. obviate

E (page 104)

1. forage
2. visage
3. credible
4. patronage
5. articulate

SEQUENCE 9-27

B (page 106)

1. b
2. a
3. b
4. a
5. b

C (page 107)

1. dialogue, a
2. catalogue, b
3. synonym, c
4. antonym, a
5. pseudonym, a

D (page 108)

1. anthology
2. dialogue
3. theology
4. catalogue
5. apology

E (page 108)

1. monologue
2. synonym
3. etymology
4. monologue
5. pseudonym

ANSWER KEY

Sequences 9-28 to 9-30

SEQUENCE 9-28

B (page 110)

1. a, b
2. b
3. a, b
4. b
5. a, b

C (page 111)

1. thermometer, b
2. pentagon, c
3. octagon, b
4. spectacular, a
5. rectangular, a

D (page 112)

1. spectacular
2. pedometer
3. chronometer
4. perimeter
5. pentagon

E (page 112)

1. thermometer
2. spectacular
3. pentagon
4. pedometer
5. triangular

SEQUENCE 9-29

B (page 114)

1. b
2. b
3. a, b
4. a
5. b

C (page 115)

1. aesthetic, b
2. antibiotic, a
3. exotic, b
4. dissimilar, c
5. symbiotic, c

D (page 116)

1. pathetic
2. curricular
3. exotic
4. aesthetic
5. phonetic

E (page 116)

1. prophetic
2. aesthetic
3. dissimilar
4. symbiotic
5. antibiotic

SEQUENCE 9-30

B (page 118)

1. b
2. b
3. a
4. b
5. a

C (page 119)

1. serenade, a
2. brackish, c
3. brandish, b
4. emphasis, c
5. prosthesis, c

D (page 120)

1. decade
2. brackish
3. devilish
4. analysis
5. emphasis

E (page 120)

1. barricade
2. devilish
3. emphasis
4. brandish
5. barricade

PROGRESS CHART

SCORE 20 POINTS FOR EACH CORRECT ANSWER IN EXERCISES D AND E.
SCORE 10 POINTS FOR EACH CORRECT ANSWER IN EXERCISE G.

(EXAMPLE)

SEQUENCE NUMBER	SEQUENCE SECTION SCORE D	E	G	PAGE NUMBER	DATE
9-1	80			4	September 12, 2004
		100		4	September 12, 2004
			90		September 15, 2004

SEQUENCE NUMBER	SEQUENCE SECTION SCORE D	E	G	PAGE NUMBER	DATE
9-1					
9-2					
9-3					

SEQUENCE NUMBER	SEQUENCE SECTION SCORE			PAGE NUMBER	DATE
	D	E	G		
9-4					
9-5					
9-6					
9-7					
9-8					
9-9					
9-10					
9-11					

SEQUENCE NUMBER	SEQUENCE SECTION SCORE			PAGE NUMBER	DATE
	D	E	G		
9-12					
9-13					
9-14					
9-15					
9-16					
9-17					
9-18					
9-19

SEQUENCE NUMBER	SEQUENCE SECTION SCORE D	SEQUENCE SECTION SCORE E	SEQUENCE SECTION SCORE G	PAGE NUMBER	DATE
9-20					
9-21					
9-22					
9-23					
9-24					
9-25					
9-26					
9-27					

SEQUENCE NUMBER	SEQUENCE SECTION SCORE D	E	G	PAGE NUMBER	DATE
9-28					
9-29					
9-30					